MARKETING ON A SHOESTRING

Low-Cost Tips for Marketing Your Products or Services

JEFFREY P. DAVIDSON

WILEY

John Wiley & Sons

New York • Chichester • Brisbane • Toronto • Singapore

Library of Congress Cataloging in Publication Data:
Davidson, Jeffrey P.
  Marketing on a shoestring.

  Bibliography: p.
  1. Marketing.   2. Marketing–Costs.   I. Title.
HF5415.D348   1988   658.8   87-29446

ISBN 0-471-63253-8
ISBN 0-471-63285-6 (pbk.)

Printed in the United States of America

10 9 8 7 6 5 4 3

To Karl Weber, Kerry Harding, Katherine Reynolds, and Holland Cook—some of the best friends an author ever had— and to my wonderful aunt and uncle, Tybe and Jiggs Mandell.

FOREWORD

Pick up any issue of *Inc.*, *Venture*, or *Business Week* and it appears as if every other person going into business is fully capitalized, able to execute a well developed marketing plan, and regularly meets revenue forecasts. Follow-up stories to those with bold, flashy headlines, however, are usually not written, or are buried inside the publication.

The fact is that the business failure rate in the late 1980s exceeds all previous years. The business failure rate has more than doubled in the last thirty years, and is more than triple the low failure rates of the 1970s.

After steering past the glitzy media barrage, the reality of the entrepreneurial experience emerges. Owning and operating a business is one of the riskiest endeavors in which an individual can engage, and is liable to consume one's savings, energy, and spirit.

Routinely, we've attended the grand opening or kick-off campaign of a new business that in a few short years ends up failing. Still, we continue to view entrepreneurism with rose colored glasses. Perhaps there is no greater myth in society today than the notion that operating your own business is guaranteed to be a desirable, fulfilling experience.

Amidst increasing failure rates, interest in starting a business is vibrant. There are now more than 14,000,000 small businesses in the United States, according to the U.S. Small Business Administration. In the last decade the number of new business startups has been at an all-time high, and this trend seems very likely to continue. Each year more than 650,000 new businesses are started. More than 3,000,000 businesses are now owned by women—more than double the number for 1975. The number of independently employed individuals will be growing dramatically for the balance of the 1990s as millions from the baby boom generation are squeezed from the corporate ranks. Millions of others are simply waiting for the moment they can leave their full-time positions to devote 100% of their time to their own ventures.

Most startup entrepreneurs, however, lack the resources and funds necessary to market their businesses in the ways that they had hoped. Their marketing plans are often fueled by a wish and a prayer. Though we live in a media driven era, effective use of the media for marketing is beyond the vast majority of entrepreneurs. Still, as social, technological, and economic changes occur, entrepreneurs face an array of new problems and challenges that will require dramatic new approaches.

In this book, Jeff Davidson's ninth, you will learn some basic low-cost strategies for marketing your business. I first met Jeff when he appeared as a guest on the television show I host for the U.S. Chamber of Commerce entitled "Ask Washington." I was immediately struck by Jeff's broad base of business knowledge and the ease and clarity with which he conveys that knowledge. I have since come to know that what he puts down on paper is worth reading.

This is more than just a book on inexpensive marketing techniques — it is an interesting and fun book. Jeff explores the effective use of the telephone, and why so many companies don't use the telephone properly; making the most of the lunch and dinner (the rubber chicken) circuit; how to make important professional contacts every time you leave your office; and why five dollars an hour still buys a lot in the form of part-time marketing help.

Whether you have just started your own business, or you have been in business for several years, you'll find *Marketing on a Shoestring* to be just what the doctor ordered to effectively market your business without paying a fortune. The recommendations and suggestions he makes are easy to understand and to follow. Jeff is not prone to dispensing advice his readers will have difficulty implementing.

As you read this book, keep in mind that there are hundreds of thousands of other entrepreneurs just like you. All are striving to make successes of their businesses while conserving precious capital. Ignore the suggestions and advice offered and you put yourself at a competitive disadvantage. Initiate these effective low-cost marketing strategies, and they will begin to pay off in a few short months.

Marketing on a Shoestring is a refreshing alternative for hundreds of thousands of entrepreneurs who need to maintain a professional image and execute an effective marketing campaign but realize that they simply don't have the funds, or, in the case of those who do, would still be happy to hear of suitable, low-cost alternatives. It offers proven, practical yet highly professional marketing strategies, techniques, and tips for an eager audience of business entrepreneurs.

As host of "Ask Washington," I am often asked where to go, or what to do, to market effectively at low cost. The underlying theme of this book is that there are low-cost alternative approaches for nearly all conventional marketing vehicles. Jeff addresses finding and using boilerplate material to promote your business, getting in newspapers without placing ads, creating reciprocal advertising, and quickly analyzing the competition.

The language he uses is simple, straight-forward, and directed towards entrepreneurs who have, at best, a rudimentary knowledge of marketing. Marketing veterans, however, will also find this book highly useful.

I hope you read this book with enthusiasm and vigor. Use it as the catalyst to spark still other ideas and strategies for marketing your business inexpensively.

LARRY BUTLER

U.S. Chamber of Commerce
Washington, DC

INTRODUCTION

This book is not just "101 low-cost ways to market your business," although more than 100 low-cost tips are offered. Rather, it focuses on basic strategies for effective marketing. *Marketing on a Shoestring* is first a frame of mind and second a set of principles for active execution.

In Chapter 1, Creative Marketing, we will discuss the importance of spending your time instead of your money to market your business. To become an effective shoestring marketer, you may need to abandon some preconceived notions. We will discuss how to profile your customers, using demographics, and the importance that your marketing presentations will have on potential customers and clients.

Chapter 2, Making It Easy on Your Customers, discusses how to name your business, products, and services so as to appeal to the target market. It also focuses on developing associates or sales staff to whom your customers and clients can relate, and stresses the important role customer service plays in marketing.

In Chapter 3, Customer Leverage Strategies, we'll focus on the value of your existing customer and client base in terms of generating long-term business and a steady stream of referrals. Your good customers want to help you and we'll discuss how to help them to help you and ways to make your customers look good. We will also focus on some simple in-house marketing assessment techniques for determining the effectiveness of current strategies and vehicles.

In Chapter 4, Marketing Through the Telephone, we will discuss telemarketing, the opportunity that you receive in every telephone inquiry, and why most businesses are not taking advantage of the tremendous marketing opportunities offered by telemarketing. We will also look at the important role your staff, and particularly your receptionist, play in the overall marketing program.

In Chapter 5, Using Part-Time Help, we will see why five dollars an hour still buys a lot and why using part-time and temporary help will be of growing importance to your business and your marketing effectiveness. We will also explore college internship programs and how they can offer a marketing shot in the arm.

Chapter 6, Yellow Page Advertising That Gets Noticed, examines some new tricks in an old but rapidly changing medium. We will demonstrate why a picture (but not a photo!) is still worth a thousand words and how you can appeal to the subconscious. We'll also discuss what makes a good ad and how to create your own with relative ease.

Chapter 7, Advertising in Business Directories, will introduce you to the most highly regarded directories among purchasing agents and industrial buyers. If you're a business-to-business entrepreneur offering durable goods, this chapter will be of great interest.

Producing high quality brochures and other marketing support items is usually expensive. In Chapter 8, Creating an Unforgettable Brochure, we'll focus on budget-conscious techniques to assure that you get maximum benefit for the money shelled out. We list the essential elements of the brochure, discuss the brochure scan, and explain how to use stock photos and to produce effective business cards. We will also examine how trade associations can help you reduce the costs of producing a high quality brochure.

Chapter 9, Strategic Bulletin Boards, surveys alternative vehicles for getting your message out, including bulletin boards, metro handbooks, directories, and highly focused smaller publications and newsletters. We'll also talk about value packs, controlled action letters, and many other strategies. Numerous examples of ads in alternative publications are provided.

Chapter 10 discusses how prospecting can be enhanced by working The Lunch and Dinner Circuit. It highlights the need to become an insider, the efforts required to prospect using this method, and how to obtain key directories and membership rosters that facilitate prospecting efforts.

In Chapter 11, Bartering and Swapping, we'll open the door to highly effective low-cost marketing strategies that have fueled the fires of many entrepreneurs. We will examine reciprocal ads, Rolodex reviews, tip clubs, and other high leverage strategies for effective shoestring marketing.

Chapter 12, Sixteen More Low-Cost Marketing Tips, offers a potpourri of ideas ranging from using college business majors to conduct free marketing surveys, to getting free publicity photos through civic groups and association memberships. It also discusses how to generate customer-related news, how to make group ads work for you, and how local business associations can pool marketing efforts.

THE LINES ARE BLURRING

The distinctions between service provider, retailer, distributor, and contractor are merging. As more and more service providers increase and diversify the range of customer services, many are beginning to offer products as well.

Conversely, retail entrepreneurs have long recognized that service during and after the sale helps build long-term customer loyalty. Thus, as you read through this book you will find it useful to review recommendations earmarked for every type of business. It is likely that some strategies and techniques used in businesses that differ from yours may apply with some modification to your own enterprise.

HOW THIS BOOK DIFFERS

There are many books available on entrepreneurship and marketing, some of which offer advice on controlling and containing marketing costs. The approach taken in *Marketing on a Shoestring* differs from existing texts in that the reader can use most of the basic strategies discussed here without any previous marketing experience.

Because cost information varies among regions and certainly among countries, and because all costs are subject to change, I mention costs sparingly. Specific costs are provided for purposes of illustration or in the case of, say, national directories when they apply across a considerable area. Also, this book provides only minimal information on direct mail, selling techniques, sales management, and other areas that have been explored thoroughly by other texts.

Marketing on a Shoestring has been prepared for the entrepreneur who wants the "real line" on practical, low-cost marketing strategies that can be read, understood, and initiated in short order.

JEFFREY P. DAVIDSON

Falls Church, Virginia
April, 1988

ACKNOWLEDGMENTS

I would like to acknowledge Katherine J. Reynolds, Louis Baron, Erin Austin, Dianne Walbrecker, Joan Pastor, Philip O'Keefe, and John McCarrier for their assistance and support. For specific contributions, thanks also go to Jon Evetts, Tony Alessandra, Bob Bly, Michael Gershman, G.A. Marken, Grace Evans, Cathy Sachs, Michael LeBouef, Cathy Bellizzi, and Mona Piontkowski. Thanks to Brenda C. Earner and Sandy Stiner for expert copyediting and proofreading.

A special note of thanks goes to Judy Dubler for her supreme, highly professional word processing support. Finally, I would like to thank Karl Weber, Richard McCullough, Peter Clifton, Arlynn Greenbaum, Steve Kippur, Ph.D., and all the fine folks at Wiley for their professionalism and unceasing efforts.

J.P.D.

CONTENTS

WILEY BOOKS BY JEFFREY P. DAVIDSON

MARKETING ON A SHOESTRING
GETTING NEW CLIENTS (with Richard A. Connor, Jr.)
MARKETING YOUR CONSULTING AND PROFESSIONAL
  SERVICES (with Richard A. Connor, Jr.)

1

CREATIVE MARKETING

The greatness of one man cannot be dictated by another. A man is a mind and a soul within a shell of flesh and bone, and no man will know anyone better than his own self. Therefore, he must first learn harmony from within, before his outward quest with fellow man can end with success.

R. Mark Morris

Despite government statistics indicating a downward trend in inflation during the 1980s, the cost of marketing has continued to rise, putting great pressure on the nation's 14 million small business owners, managers, and entrepreneurs. In a media driven society riches accrue to those parties able to dominate or make the best use of television, radio, newspapers, and major magazines.

A quick examination of the cost of using major media to market a business, however, reveals that for virtually all start-up companies, many companies in existence for a few years, and untold numbers of older businesses, these vehicles are out of range. A one half-page, two-color advertisement in a local or regional magazine such as the *Bostonian, Warfield's,* or *Dallas* averages $2600. A full-page ad, black and white, in *Female Executive* costs $3540. One two-column by six-inch advertisement in the *Chicago Sun Times* or the *Denver Post* starts at approximately $2000. A 30-second TV spot, nonprime time in a midsized metro area such as Des Moines still sets you back $1500—for just one airing!

Today, any type of consistent marketing effort using these media vehicles would require running your ad at least four to six times. The dollars add up quickly. Suppose your business serves a local market and less grandiose measures, such as brochures and catalogs, will suffice to market your business. A well-developed brochure or catalog, employing four-color graphics on quality paper, can average $150 per hour plus costs, or a minimum of $1000 per page, not including the cost of printing copies.

And so it goes down the line. Yellow Pages advertisements, store signs, logos and stationery, and even business cards require the outlay of significant sums, and this can leave the entrepreneur feeling that when it comes to the cost of marketing, there is nowhere to turn.

MARKETING DURING START-UP

Compounding the marketing difficulties faced by start-up entrepreneurs, upon introducing a product or service, the entrepreneur is faced with even greater marketing challenges as he or she tries to gain visibility in a selected target niche and build market share.

According to Booz, Allen and Hamilton, an international management consulting firm, there are four stages in the life cycle of a retail business. During the first six months of operation, a business can expect to reach roughly half of its full sales potential. The *introductory* phase may not necessarily occur within the first six months of operations; however, six months is used as a benchmark.

The next phase is *growth*, which generally occurs between the sixth and the twenty-fourth month of operations. During the growth stage, a business can expect to achieve roughly 65% to 70% of its full sales potential. As with the introductory stage, the growth phase may be shortened or extended, based on the particular business and industry being observed.

The third phase of the retail cycle, *maturity*, occurs between the second and fourth year of operation. In the mature stage, a business can achieve its complete sales potential, a level based on industry trends, sales per square foot, or other measures. A business can remain in the mature phase for several years.

During the last phase, *decline*, a business may continue to show profits as either net sales or net profitability begins to decline or as the industry in which the business operates experiences a sharp decline.

The sales cycle above is not recognized by many entrepreneurs. Many, still in the growth stage, strive to achieve a sales level that is attainable only in the mature phase.

While new businesses often face the urgent need to market themselves effectively during the introductory and growth phases, this is also the time in which cash flow may become restricted. Many an entrepreneur is forced to dig into monies that had been allocated for marketing and promotion. In working with over 225 businesses since 1975, I have observed that when spending cuts must be made by the entrepreneur, unfortunately, they are apt to occur in the area of marketing.

This book is geared to first-time as well as veteran entrepreneurs who recognize that a well-planned, ongoing, highly targeted marketing program is a necessity of business life, regardless of how expensive traditional marketing vehicles become.

CASTING TOO WIDE A NET

Perhaps the single greatest marketing mistake that I have observed, even among entrepreneurs who have allocated sufficient funds or who recognize the need to continually attract new customers, is the failure to clearly define the market to be served. Thus, an underlying principle of effective shoestring marketing is ensuring that the time, energy, and dollars you do spend on marketing are focused on the targeted group(s) you see as key to the success of your business.

Your targets should have needs that you can readily meet at a profit. It sounds basic, yet I still encounter entrepreneurs who target six to eight different groups and then produce six to eight different versions of their brochure. You must focus your energies if you expect to maintain a solid reputation as an entrepreneur. Whether it is MacDonald's and its golden arches; Colonel Sanders, "We do chicken, just chicken"; or Wisk, "Wisk fights ring around the collar", successful national advertisers have long recognized that the quickest way to marketing effectiveness is to consistently deliver a message that establishes the company, product, or service in the minds of the target market.

If you were quizzed right now as to what business you are in or what your company is known for, what would the answer be? If the answer is long and involved, then you haven't properly positioned your product and/or service. Today's consumer—including your best potential customers or clients—must contend with an unprecedented amount of information. Whether you sell to other businesses or to individual consumers, your ability to rise above the marketing din rests squarely on your ability to establish an image. Even retail store owners, who are heavily dependent upon location, nevertheless must establish themselves in a manner similar to that of business or professional service providers or national product distributors.

Cast too wide a net and any marketing efforts you undertake, at any cost, will suffer from the inherent inefficiency of trying to be something to everyone, or too much to too many. Focus on key groups that you can readily and profitably serve, and shoestring marketing techniques will pay off.

Using Your Time Instead of Your Money

You can market effectively without shelling out large chunks of money. Here is a simple exercise to illustrate that creative approaches to the marketplace need not be expensive.

If you have been in business for a year or more, list your 10 best customers or clients. If you are a start-up entrepreneur, create a hypothetical list of the 10 best customers or clients. In reviewing this list, consider what these targets:

☐ **Read**. Do they read the local newspaper or more targeted industry journals? Do they receive professional and trade newsletters? Are they more inclined to read consumer magazines? Or, generally speaking, do they not read?

☐ **Attend**. Do your targets attend national conventions and trade shows? Do they participate in civic and community events accessible to you? What do they attend regularly, and why?

□ **Respond to**. Does this group respond to phone calls, letters, on-site visits? How did they first hear of you? Why have they stayed with you?

□ **Must overcome**. How well do you know the problems of your target market? How can you gather information on the problems they face?

The better you know the customers or clients, the better you can serve their needs and the better you will be able to inexpensively attract other clients with similar needs. You can't sufficiently execute a low-cost marketing program unless you have a comprehensive understanding of the needs, fears, and passions of those you would serve.

If you worked in the businesses or lived in the homes of those representing your target market, you would immediately see many ways of reaching them. Short of working for them or living with them, you must learn to tap into the minds of your targets. How is this done? Read what they read, attend what they attend, keep notes on their responses, and talk to them about their problems.

MORE BUSINESS, BETTER PROFITABILITY— THE NAME OF THE GAME

There are two ways to increase profits: generate greater revenues while keeping all other costs in line, or reduce costs while maintaining revenues. Of course, a combination of the two also will yield an improved profit picture. Shoestring marketing reduces some costs of marketing. For the $8000 or more you might have paid for six ads (all media offer volume discounts) in your area's regional magazine, you can initiate a super shoestring marketing program, leveraging existing resources for maximum gain.

A few months or years into the business, many entrepreneurs become undercapitalized and overanxious. As revenue projections prove to be inaccurate and financial management transforms into checkbook management, there is a tendency to go for the big marketing score. Among contractors, this is characterized by attempting to land the one big job that is going to put the company back in shape. Among retailers, this appears as the Christmas or other big holiday sale that will salvage previous losses. Among professional service providers, this takes the form of fantasy—a bevy of attractive, prosperous clients with unending needs are just about to retain our services.

The importance of shoestring marketing techniques for the new, undercapitalized, or unprofitable entrepreneur cannot be overemphasized. Accomplishing marketing goals while avoiding the outlay of large expenditures to achieve those goals greatly increases the probability of your long-term survival.

Handing over thousands of dollars to support some media representative in the hopes that you can avoid establishing a creative, evolving marketing program generally results in:

☐ swift reduction of the "dear dollars"—initial working capital that you had earmarked for marketing, and

☐ the realization that your remaining resources will have to suffice.

Start Early

From the beginning, why not establish a program of inexpensive strategies and vehicles for accomplishing your marketing goals? In the end, it will probably come to that, anyway. If shoestring marketing is part of a consistent, preplanned effort, then the panic and anxiety that plagues so many others need not affect you.

Speak with any start-up entrepreneur and you will hear glowing revenue projections. Invariably, these goals are not achieved. Why not approach shoestring marketing as the appropriate course of action from the beginning rather than relying upon shoestring techniques as a necessity following the failure of an expensive marketing program?

If you're concerned that undertaking shoestring marketing will cast your business in a bad light, fear not. The strategies and information presented throughout this book are for your eyes only. If executed properly, your targets will give little thought to the way in which they were attracted to your business versus those of your competitors making large cash outlays. In fact, because many shoestring approaches require a personal touch or cast your business in a unique light, you may find that your products and services are perceived as superior to those offered by competitors with the dollars to pay for heavy marketing artillery.

Sticking to Your Guns When the Clouds Look Gray

I pointed out in my earlier book, *Marketing to the Fortune 500* (Homewood, IL: Dow Jones-Irwin, 1987), that the typical entrepreneur calling upon the purchasing department of a large corporation for the first time erroneously believes the time necessary to consummate a contract following an initial meeting averages two months. However, discussion with several corporate purchasing agents, as well as veteran small business contractors, reveals that the average time in which a sale is consummated is closer to 18 months—nine times the time expectation of entrepreneurs!

I don't know if the "nine times factor" applies in all lines of businesses and professions. However, I frequently have observed that the inability to reasonably estimate the time required to generate new business is pervasive among entrepreneurs. If you are eager to initiate a shoestring marketing program, a proper time perspective must be established as for any type of marketing program. When the projected results are not achieved on schedule, the projections usually were far too optimistic.

Fortitude and consistency are the watchwords of the effective shoestring marketer. So you don't achieve your initial projections—you still may have some significant achievements. In this day of information overload and increased foreign competition, if you remain a reliable, visible product or service provider, the rewards will come your way, and no other course will work better in the short or long run.

PROFILING YOUR CUSTOMERS

To keep your customers, you must satisfy them. You must know who they are and what they need. In other words, you must study them. However, an effective study involves more than just informal conversation.

There are two major sources of information needed to keep abreast of your customers' needs.

You can collect primary data by keeping tabs on customer or client activity. For example, you can determine which credit cards are being used, how frequently your clients are calling, what types of merchandise or services are selling the fastest, and the proportions of race/gender/age/income level of your customers.

You can also collect primary data on an intended target market: where they reside, their income levels, how many children they have, and so on. When profiling your customers, however, never make assumptions. The business environment is constantly in motion. Failure is due largely to incorrect assumptions about customer needs. Primary data on your competitors increases your ability to compete effectively.

Secondary data is collected by other sources. You can subscribe to pertinent magazines such as *American Demographics, Sales and Marketing Management, U.S. News and World Report, Future,* and *Public Opinion,* which publish useful charts and follow trends. You can write to research and information services such as the U.S. Bureau of the Census, Washington, D.C. 20233, or the American Marketing Association, 250 S. Wacker Drive, Suite 200, Chicago, IL 60606.

The advantages of secondary data are that it is quick and inexpensive to collect. The main disadvantage is that it may be too general or dated for your specific needs.

Demographics

Demographics are used to identify and categorize a target population. The U.S. Bureau of the Census collects data on the general population in several key areas. Let's briefly review highlights in eight key areas, as noted by Professors Joel Evans and Barry Berman in their book *Marketing* (New York: Macmillan, 1986, 2nd edition).

1. *Age.* As a result of longer life spans, the U.S. population is getting older. The median age in the U.S. is now 33 years old and 12% of the population is over 65. Products and services

geared toward this more mature market are growing rapidly. You can use in-house tabulations to determine the primary age groups you serve.

2. *Gender.* In 1980, there were 6 million more females than males in the United States. There also has been a huge increase in the number of working women during the past decade. Products and services including life insurance, financial planning, condominium resorts, and racquetball equipment, previously reserved for men, are now routinely marketed to women, too.

3. *Occupation.* The U.S. Bureau of Labor Statistics predicts that the labor force will continue to become more white-collar and service-oriented, and blue-collar and agricultural industries will move to lesser developed countries. This trend will have a great impact on the goods and services in demand in the future.

4. *Education.* Better educated consumers and clients will demand to know more about the products and services offered and will take less for granted. A person's occupation is often (but not always) a fair indicator of his level of education.

5. *Marital Status.* Marriage and divorce rates have several marketing implications. First, because more women are working, more married couples have two incomes. This allows greater purchasing power. At the same time, an increasing number of divorcees now buys the goods and services that previously were shared with a spouse.

6. *Income and Expenditures.* As the number of two-income families rises, so do disposable incomes and consumer expenditures. Income and expenditure information is readily available in annual issues of business magazines, such as *Sales and Marketing Management*, and in numerous government reports.

7. *Location.* The population in the United States continues to migrate to the south and west. Where are the majority of your customers or clients located? This information can be obtained from sales receipts or customer mailing lists. If they are all local, can you find ways to make it worth someone's time to travel a little farther to buy your product, or would greater penetration of your primary trade area make more sense?

8. *Housing and Mobility.* Do your customers or clients own their own homes? Do they rent apartments? Do they have large yards? Will their jobs keep them in town for several years? The answers to these questions can tell you which types of goods or services will be in the greatest demand.

Customer Psychographics

Not all people in similar demographic categories react in the same way to all situations or have the same wants and needs. Psychographics break down demographics one step further by considering a consumer's social and psychological characteristics, which create a unique lifestyle. You must analyze lifestyles in order to create a clearer picture of your client base.

A current example of the need for psychographics was illustrated in attempts to define Middle America. A few decades ago this group was perhaps one of the best defined target groups in the country. This is no longer true. Middle America is so fragmented that Ray Albondi, marketing research director at Ford Motor Company, stated, "We don't recognize something called a middle class. We use as many as 200 or 300 different measurement points to identify our customer." That's far too many measurement points for you to use.

Can you accurately assess the group(s) to whom you sell? If so, your marketing efforts will be greatly enhanced.

2

MAKING IT EASY ON YOUR CUSTOMERS

The key to success is unknown, but the key to failure is trying to please everybody.

Bill Cosby

Making it easy for the customer to find your business or be attracted to your products or services, relate to your sales staff or associates, and be served by your company will go a long way in supporting your marketing efforts. Let's examine each of these areas in detail.

SELECTING YOUR COMPANY NAME

The task of picking an appropriate name for your company or for your product is a huge responsibility. With just a few words, your name must conjure up an attractive image and it also must distinguish you from your competition. A name that's right on target is a marketing necessity. A name that's not well-chosen can become a marketing stumbling block.

Choosing company names is big business itself. Millions of dollars are paid annually to consultants who specialize in picking names. The U.S. Patent and Trademark Office has registered more than 150,000 new trade names in the past four years, double the number registered in the previous four years.

Some large international firms are so well known that their company name is firmly etched in the minds of those they are trying to reach. Examples include: Booz, Allen & Hamilton in consulting; Planning Research Corporation (PRC), a diversified services firm; and Peat Marwick & Main (PMM), one of the "Big Eight" public accounting firms.

For less familiar firms, however, the use of certain combinations of words in the name can be confusing. For example, the words *management, resource,* and *systems* when strung together could be the name of a firm entitled Management Resource Systems, Resource Management Systems, or Systems Management Resources.

Listed below are words commonly used in company names that can be confusing to the target market. (This list, incidentally, in no way implies that these words should not be in your company's name, but using combinations of these words may confuse potential clients.)

executive	American	research
opportunity	planning	data
computer	profession or	consultants
international	professional	resource(s)
management	advance(d)	systems
corporation	applied	counsel
corporate	planner	information
institute	industrial	specialists
center	national	organization
operations	group	technology
specialists	search	interface
united	analysis	

American Research Technology doesn't sound bad, but who are they? Advanced Planning Systems, Research and Management Analysis, Applied Industrial Development, Computer Technology Systems, National Data Analysts, Applied Management Corporation, Information Systems Planners, National Planners and Technology Consultants, Applied Technology Resources Group,

Computer Systems Corporation, and The Center for Operations Analysis similarly do not stand out.

In all, there are more than 25,000 different three-word combinations that can be created using the above list, most of which produce a professional-sounding, semantically appropriate, yet indistinguishable business name. Large firms such as General Research Corporation (GRC), Electronic Data System (EDS), and the Urban Land Institute (ULI) can get away with using these words and even use acronyms ("alphabet soup"). Smaller firms need to be very careful, as this most definitely affects marketing efforts.

Using the Founder's Surname

Examining the older, established firms within consulting reveals that at least one founder's surname is always a part of the company name. For example, McKinsey & Company; George S. May International; Lawrence Leiter & Associates; and Theodore Barry Associates. Only a few of the members of ACME, the Association of Consulting Management Engineers, do not include at least one surname within their title, such as, the Middle West Service Company, headquartered in Chicago. For a new or young firm entering consulting, to better establish the firm's identity within the market place, the surname of a founder or a principal of the company should be used as part of the company's name.

The most widely required marketing research and public opinion polls are the Gallup Poll, named after George Gallup; the Harris Poll, named after Louis Harris; and Yankelovich, Skelly and White, Inc. Within advertising agencies, the names of successful firms involve use of surnames of the principals or founders. This is true in the case of Young and Rubicam International; Wells, Rich & Greene; and the Walter J. Thompson Company. This trend is also maintained among public relations firms. Consider Burson-Marsteller; Daniel J. Edelman, Inc.; and Hill and Knowlton.

For high-tech companies, a different strategy is appropriate (see below).

It's not necessary to hire an expensive consultant to create an appropriate name. If you know your company, its products and services, and the specific audience you want to reach, you can create effective names.

Gather the Basic Information

To begin, you'll need to describe what you are naming, define your target audience, and list the names of your competitors. Salinon Corporation, a naming consulting firm, headquartered in Greenville, Texas recommends the following six steps.

Describe What You Are Naming. What is it that makes your product or service different? What can you do better than all your competitors? What features does your product include? How will your services save your client time, money, and anxiety? Clarifying this information will be useful to you in choosing the right name as well as in other areas of marketing.

Summarize What You Would Like the Name to Accomplish. From the descriptions you have just written, which features would you like the name to convey? Close your eyes and imagine the effect that your name will have on consumers. What connotation does it carry? How does the name make a person feel? Most importantly, what experiences can be linked favorably with your product or service?

Define Your Audience. Market definition is vital for all aspects of your company's development. Which groups do you want to target for your product or service and what type of name would appeal to them? Are they older people trying to act young? Are they city dwellers longing for a simpler lifestyle? List the qualities your audience would find attractive in a name and those they probably would dislike. For example, older people trying to act young will react differently to certain words:

Attractive	*Unattractive*
Bouncy	Stable
Vibrant	Secure
Energetic	Comfortable
Dynamic	Steadfast
Spontaneous	Fixed

Zestful	Rooted
New	Dependable
Flashy	Mature

List Names You Like and Dislike. Find a dozen or more names that evoke a strong reaction in you, either positive or negative. You can go outside your field to find these names, but you must strongly like or dislike them. Then analyze your reaction to each name, searching for common roots, phrases, length, sounds, letters, or any other similarities.

Write Down Your Competitors' Names. Discover what you like and what you dislike about the names your competitors have chosen. Is there a pattern among their names, a certain length of name or root that many of them use? For example, among copier companies, names include:

Xerox	Ricoh
Kodak	Panasonic
Cannon	Konica
IBM	Sharp
Toshiba	Minolta
Sanyo	Harris
Savin	A-Copy

All names are two or more syllables, and many have hard consonant sounds like K and R. Kodak, Xerox, Ricoh, and Konica fit this pattern particularly well. Maybe you could call your new copier Corika, or Sanika.

Will breaking away from the established naming pattern set you apart as a vibrant newcomer or as an unruly spoiler? Analyze what their names communicate and how different words, phrases, and sounds can convey varying images.

Identify the Type of Name You Want. Using a completely unknown word for your name has the advantage of avoiding confusion with any other name, but it may require costly advertising to establish identity. Bypass this problem by making up a word from real words or roots. A name like "Plant High" has natural connotations, making it less costly to establish.

A single or multiple real word name can lead to useful, descriptive names, but be careful. A name that is too descriptive cannot be trademarked. A name where each letter represents a more descriptive word or phrase is short and easily remembered. Using personal names or place names is acceptable, according to the Salinon Corporation, but they, too, are difficult to trademark.

Building Your Name—Part and Synonym List

Now, divide a piece of paper into four columns. In columns one and four, list any generic phrases or words that you will always want in your name. For instance, if you're naming a consulting firm and you want your surname at the beginning of the company's name, put it in the first column. You've always liked the sound of "and Associates" and would like that at the end of your company name, so list that in the fourth column. However, leave columns one and four blank if you have no fixed words or phrases to use.

Next, review the list of names you liked and disliked. In its booklet *The Naming Guide*, Salinon lists generic roots and words used in the majority of names introduced today. They recommend adding some of the more appropriate ones, those which will combine well with columns one and four, to your worksheets. Using columns two and three of the table on p. 17, if you've already chosen parts for columns one and four, list any part or name that you like and that you feel might work for your company.

Some examples of companies that had preselected choices for the opening and closing words or roots in the names they ultimately chose are shown on p. 18.

Verify Name Availability and Test the Name

Another important part of the naming process is to check your choices for undesirable connotations, especially if you are serving any non-English-speaking markets. According to Salinon, the naming business abounds with stories of naming snafus: the large oil

Salinon Generic Root List

ab	edge	guard	max	puls	tel
ac	eke	halo	meg	pur	ter
ace	end	hard	mer	quest	term
act	equa	harvest	micro	quik	tip
acu	ers	helm	mind	race	ton
age	ets	help	mine	re	touch
aim	ever	hi	mira	ref	tr
aliv	ex	hol	mod	ris	tra
all	exp	icks	mult	rite	trans
amaz	extra	ier	my	rose	tron
amer	fab	im	net	sag	tru
an	feast	in	new	sav	tune
auto	fect	inc	now	score	typ
ba	fest	inter	nu	seed	ultra
bel	fiber	ize	nutra	self	un
ben	find	jet	o	sen	up
best	fine	joy	oasis	serve	usa
bet	firm	key	omni	set	val
bond	first	lab	ord	shield	valet
boost	fit	lax	pa	site	vault
bred	flash	lead	pac	smart	vect
bud	flex	leaf	pace	so	ven
ca	flo	lean	pal	source	via
cap	focus	let	pan	spir	vig
car	fox	lif	paq	spri	vip
cater	free	lift	path	spring	vision
chief	fresh	line	pep	sprout	viv
co	front	link	per	st	ware
comf	gain	lit	perm	star	way
comp	gate	li	pioneer	store	wealth
con	gem	lock	plex	steam	well
corp	gize	log	plus	struct	whiz
cosm	glo	lov	ply	su	wit
cur	global	ma	po	sun	wonder
day	go	macra	pop	super	works
de	gold	marc	pr	sur	world
di	gon	mast	pre	sync	x
dur	good	master	prim	sys	xon
dyn	grip	mate	pro	team	zap
easi	gro	matic	prov	tek	zip

Constructing a Business Name*

	Column 1	Column 2	Column 3	Column 4
a		MICRO	SOFT	
b		DYN	O	METER
c		PRO	SERVE	
d	THE	COSM	IC	BAKERY
e	LANDMARK	COMPUTER	LABS	INC
f		PERM	A	LENS
g		SERVICE	MASTER	
h	INTER	STATE	OFFICE	SUPPLY
i		MASTER	MIND	
j	VALET	IN	A	CAN
k		TEK	TRON	IC
l		SURFA	SHIELD	INSTITUTE
m		HARVEST	HOUSE	
n	SEN	SO	DINE	
o		DAY	GLO	PAINTS
p	LIGHT	AND	EASY	

* All are actual names of business entities or products.

company that picked a name meaning "intestines" in one language; a fast-food chain that used a word referring to "big breasts" in another language. They recommend checking your name against the *International Dictionary of Obscenities* by Christina Kunitskaya-Peterson (Berkeley, CA: Berkeley Slavic, 1981).

Once you know that your name isn't obscene somewhere in the world, it is time to conduct some research. The least expensive and still suitable method is to ask friends and customers to rate your choice:

- □ Do they like it?
- □ Do they think it's a good name for your company/product/ service, or does it remind them of something else?
- □ What images or connotations do they associate with it? You'll be amazed at some of the things others associate with your name that you never considered.

□ Are these other connotations desirable?

□ Do most people pick up on the desired connotations or images?

□ Do they pronounce it correctly?

□ Can they spell it easily?

□ Can they remember it? Do they get it confused with any other existing names?

At this point you can either hire a trademark and patent attorney or conduct the trade name search on your own. Check availability at both the state and national levels by calling or writing the Patent and Trademark Office, U.S. Department of Commerce, Washington, DC 20231, (202) 557-3061. Several companies maintain federal and state trademark databases. Check your local library or telephone book for their names. Fees and turn-around times vary by company.

Choosing your company name is a major responsibility, but it can be done effectively and inexpensively. Breaking the task into the steps described above will help you discover a catchy, winning name for your company or its products and services and make it easier for your customers to identify your business.

SALES STAFF AKIN TO CUSTOMER

A second way to make it "easy on your customers" is to offer sales or staff help to whom customers can readily relate.

The first few minutes of any encounter with a customer or client are extremely important. First impressions often determine the reception that a sales pitch will receive. For this reason—and many others—it is necessary to support your product or service with a well-trained, appropriate sales force. But in order to achieve this, you must go one step beyond normal selling and training techniques. You must develop a sales force that is akin to your customer, and you must convey this same aura of kinship through any advertisements or promotions you sponsor.

You need salespeople to whom the customer can relate easily and who fit the stereotype associated with your goods or services.

The benefits of this sales technique are numerous. The primary benefit is quite simply that it works!

Healthy People Sell Health Spa Memberships

If at all possible, use salespeople who literally embody the product or service you are offering. How many times have you walked into an automotive garage and found the service manager wearing a suit and tie and speaking the King's English? Would you feel comfortable if he (or she!) did? Would you buy a pair of running shoes from an out-of-shape chain smoker? Neither of these scenarios would encourage customer faith in the sales representative or his product.

For this reason, it pays to choose salespeople who actually personify your goods and services. Visit a specialty clothing store and you will find the sales team dressed and groomed in a way that illustrates the mood and style of their inventory. In Banana Republic stores, for example, you will find personnel dressed and ready for an elephant hunt, equipped with everything from safari hats to boots—precisely the merchandise they sell.

Holiday Spas now sponsors a widely publicized campaign using celebrity representatives. Actress Heather Locklear, former "Miss Olympia" Rachel McLish, and five-time All-Pro football player Mark Gastineau are featured in several of Holiday Spas' print and television ads (see Figure 2-1). Although Rachel and Mark's large sizes may be intimidating to some, the ads suggest that the sky is the limit, and it is up to the customer "to develop the body you have always wanted."

Many companies have created individuals to star in their advertisements. For example, a recent Purolator Products campaign featured a "spokes dude" to sell Purolator automotive filters. "Duke" and his friend "Cookie" discussed their "Philosophy of Filter Fitness," using a combination of streetwise lingo and humor to reach the target audience. This ad campaign successfully utilized the "sales staff akin to the customer" concept by supplying both the atmosphere and the dialogue that appeals to do-it-yourself auto buffs.

4-MONTH SUMMER SHAPE-UP!

Sizzling Special!

A 4-Month Special Membership.*

Not looking for a long-term commitment?
How about a 4-month Holiday membership — just in time for swimsuit season.
Join Holiday Spas right now and your membership includes:

☐ **Exercise Machines from Nautilus, Universal and Paramount**
☐ **Circuit Weight Training**
☐ **Padded Indoor Jogging Tracks**
☐ **Swimming Pools**
☐ **Aerobics**
☐ **Saunas**
☐ **Whirlpools**

All that plus certified instructors and Holiday's 28 years of experience in the fitness industry. But, you've got to call Holiday now for this special 4-month membership.

holiday spas

Figure 2-1. Your company's staff and representatives should reflect your customers—or your customers' ideal image of themselves. Reprinted with permission.

Make the Most of Every Encounter

One of the keys to low-cost marketing is making the most of every encounter with a customer. The reward? Cost effectiveness. Not only will sales and customer confidence increase, but your average cost per encounter will decrease. A greater degree of quality from the sales force leads to a higher sales ratio which, in turn, translates into higher productivity. This results in lower costs per encounter and greater cost effectiveness.

According to sales trainer Jim Cathcart, professional salesmanship requires several basic qualities:

1. *Image.* As mentioned previously, first impressions are lasting and can make or break a sale. Make sure your sales force makes a positive first impression by emphasizing dress and grooming as well as personality, attitude, and body language that says, "I am a competent and confident person."

2. *Depth of Knowledge.* It is not enough to know only the basics of your specific products or services. It is necessary to dig deep into your field and industry so that you can honestly and competently answer any and all questions pitched to you. In the process, you will earn the respect and trust of your customers.

3. *Sensitivity.* Use empathy and body language to your utmost advantage to make the customer feel comfortable. Be receptive to all signs—both verbal and nonverbal—and react accordingly. Every customer needs to feel understood or he or she will go elsewhere for a more sensitive and perceptive salesperson.

4. *Enthusiasm.* The customer must believe that you and your staff are 100% behind your products or services. Why should he or she invest in something that you would not invest in yourself? Enthusiasm is the key to believability and trust.

5. *Maturity.* In this context, maturity is synonymous with responsibility or, perhaps, the acceptance of responsibility. A mature salesperson is competent and dependable. Your customer will feel confident that his or her account is being handled by someone who is willing to stay on top of things and maintain a consistent level of service.

6. *Professionalism.* Professionalism is achieved when the salesperson uses all of the above qualities to present herself as a versatile and knowledgeable individual with a clear vision of what she wants and where she wants to go.

Marketing Presentations

All presentations should be monitored periodically by management and should be consistent with the overall strategy of the organization. You must ensure that your salespeople have been groomed into sales professionals to the degree that suits your organization.

To enhance customer stability, train your sales team to promote a uniform image so the customer always knows what to expect. This may entail the development of a loose script or a set of standard greeting procedures for your sales force to follow; however, they certainly should not sound like recordings.

If it is part of your strategy to approach a customer or client as soon as he enters the store or office, then this policy should be followed for every customer. Likewise, if it is your policy to let the customer browse for a while or wait until she asks for help, then generally all of your salespeople should act accordingly.

To illustrate consistency with overall strategy, let's look at McDonald's customer greeting procedure. What is the first thing that happens when you walk into an empty McDonald's restaurant? You are immediately asked, "May I take your order?" Although some people may feel irritated and rushed by this approach, it is consistent with McDonald's overall objective to quickly serve as many people as possible.

STRICT RULES OF CUSTOMER SERVICE

Michael Baber is president of Baber Industries and a principal in the consulting and training organization Michael Baber and Associates of La Jolla, California. Baber points out that in the late 1970s, a study was performed for the White House Office of Consumer Affairs by a consulting company called Technical Assistance Research Programs, Inc. Their study indicated that on the average, for every customer who complains, there are 26 who are unhappy but do not complain. Also, the average unhappy customer tells ten other people about his dissatisfaction. Therefore, for every complaint your company actually receives, there may be as many as

260 people who know that you have performed poorly and may hesitate to do business with your company.

Here is Baber's list of 25 customer service mistakes, taken from his book *Integrated Business Leadership through Cross Marketing* (St. Louis: Warren H. Green, Inc., 1986):

1. Being unappreciative
2. Not being interested
3. Not listening
4. Unfriendliness
5. Lack of empathy
6. Ignoring customer input
7. Not asking questions
8. Forgetting customer benefits
9. Jumping the gun
10. Lack of sympathy
11. Keeping customers waiting
12. Being pushy
13. Being discourteous
14. Arguing with customers
15. Not admitting you are wrong
16. Allowing distractions
17. Rushing the customers
18. Being insensitive to behavioral styles (everyone is a little different. How do you treat punk rockers?)
19. Being undependable
20. Being inconsistent
21. Allowing them to be embarrassed
22. Criticizing customers
23. Becoming angry
24. Expecting customers to be fair
25. Wasting customer's time

To improve a company's performance, Baber designed a 15-part customer services assessment.

1. What is the most important task for me or my people to complete in the next 30 days? Why is that task the most important? How do I plan to accomplish it? How does it tie into the corporate mission or objective? What will happen as a result of it being completed?

2. Which three customer departments or divisions benefit the most from what I or my people do? How do they benefit? How could I increase the benefit to them?

3. What are the biggest problems or challenges presently facing customers?

4. When did we last ask them, by personal interview or survey, what they most want from us?

5. Which job behavior is most important to the commercial customers and to the internal departments we serve?

6. How do they rate our behavior and ability to provide results?

7. As my people or I encounter our customers and associates on a daily basis, what are the most important recurring events that give them reason to judge our service highly or poorly?

8. Compared to competitors or other associates, in what areas do our customers judge us to be strongest and weakest?

9. Which strengths or resources could we employ even more effectively to accomplish more and thus benefit those whom we serve?

10. Which single objective could I accomplish that would most benefit my company and/or my commercial customers and that would bring positive recognition to me and to my department or organization?

11. What could I do to help my people be more effective and receive more recognition?

12. What are three instances in the past week when I could have (or did) recognize the positive performance of one of my people or a fellow employee?

13. How do I communicate with commercial customers? What specific events cause me to communicate with them? Which channels (phone, mail, salesperson, etc.) do I use, and which are most effective? How do I define *effective?*

14. What could we do to improve our relationship with customers and make them even happier with our company?

15. What is the single most important action I can take to encourage my people to be more concerned with effective customer service?

This is a comprehensive assessment. I doubt there is a company out there that can't find at least a couple of areas in which improvements are warranted.

The effects of customer service are long lasting, says John Tschohl, nationally known customer service authority and president of the Better Than Money Corporation in Bloomington, Minnesota. Tschohl says, "Customer service is so obvious and so simple that it's invisible to competitors. They overlook it." He points out that many companies advertise customer service, but few actually practice it.

In closing this chapter, here are Baber's rules of customer service — the real secret to shoestring marketing. Make the customer feel:

☐ Heard.

☐ Understood.

☐ Liked.

☐ Respected.

☐ Appreciated and remembered.

☐ Helped.

3

CUSTOMER LEVERAGE STRATEGIES

A good plan today is better than a great plan tomorrow.

General George Patton

To make shoestring marketing work effectively, you must get maximum leverage from the clients and customers you presently serve as well as others whom you encounter. In our book, *Marketing Your Consulting and Professional Services* (New York: Wiley, 1985), Richard A. Connor, Jr. and I define *leverage* as the process of identifying and capitalizing on the smallest number of actions that produce the greatest results. You must constantly be aware of opportunities to gain new customer and client leads when interacting with existing customers and clients.

MINING FOR GOLD

Joan Pastor is a trainer and consultant in Del Mar, California who undertook a strategic analysis of her practice to determine the origin of most of her business. The answer was referrals.

Looking back on her business, Pastor first discovered the magic of referrals eight years ago as a practicing psychotherapist. Her first client loved her work and referred three of her friends to her. As

Pastor relates it, she took this as a matter of course. She also had been giving seminars and was gaining clients from this as well as from her private practice.

Over the years, Pastor developed and refined some specific strategies for obtaining and making the most of client referrals. In her own observation, the first thing she had to do was to change her attitude about referrals. Instead of being a passive recipient of good referrals, waiting for them to "fall out of the sky," she became an active referral seeker.

Your Good Customers and Clients Want to Help You

Here are five basic strategies that Pastor developed on the fine art of getting referrals. The principles and recommendations presented apply regardless of the product or service that you offer.

1. *Build a good foundation with your [customers or] clients by serving them well and developing a solid relationship.*

Discuss your client's needs and set specific goals. It is difficult to ask for referrals when you are concerned with the client's assessment of you. Once you have set goals with your client, show how you can achieve them. Then do it. When you get clear results, your clients can speak concretely and specifically to others about what you've accomplished.

A good working relationship grows out of good service. It is your responsibility to maintain it. Be aware that not all people require the same things in order to feel satisfied. Some like having you keep in touch by phone, while others prefer fewer calls but enjoy receiving interesting articles they can use in their business. Find out what they like. Nurture your clients.

Pastor tells her clients and prospects up front that she is looking forward to working with them and their company on a long-term basis, especially when it involves training and consulting. Even when she gives a keynote speech, she talks to several employees in the company beforehand to gather current information. It's a little extra effort, but it pays dividends in continuing business and in-house referrals.

2. *Let your client know up front you will be asking for referrals.*

Let the client know that you will be talking to her about referrals periodically. Carefully explain why you put an emphasis on referrals by outlining how your profession depends on word-of-mouth and concrete recommendations. Most people understand this and are willing to help, especially after you have helped them.

It is possible to use referrals as a tool when negotiating a contract. Speaker Lee Shapiro fell into this method unexpectedly and has had wonderful results. A client was unable to match Lee's stated fee, but he really wanted him to speak. Lee suggested that they look for a way to make this a win-win situation. The client offered to send glowing recommendation letters to every branch in the corporation at his own expense. Lee would be given the names to follow up. Lee agreed that this was a sound "marketing expansion opportunity" worth the barter. He also asked his client for a written agreement to avoid any misunderstanding.

3. *Ask for referrals and be sensitive to proper timing.*

Asking can be a hard thing to do. We're generally so uncomfortable with it that we don't ask or we ask too much too aggressively at inappropriate times. It takes practice and experience to ask for referrals effectively. The key is proper preparation of the client and good timing, which depends on the situation, the client, and your own style.

When you finish your job and they like your work, that is the time to ask, "Do you know of other branches in your company that would benefit from this, too?" The time to ask is when everyone is still interested in you. If the client is receptive to your request, also ask for a glowing testimonial letter—one that the client would feel comfortable sending (or having you send) to new contacts.

4. *Tell your client specifically what you want him to do, and follow through with him to make sure it is done properly.*

Most clients want to help you. But they will get confused and even irritated if you don't tell them clearly how they can help. First, set aside specific times with the client to talk about referrals. Tell the client that there are two areas from which referrals usually are obtained: a) those within the company who might be interested in my work, and b) those in other companies.

Discuss individuals whom they know might fit into these categories. At this point, the client may offer to make a contact for you. Ask for a commitment, and let him know you will be in touch regarding this opportunity. Don't ask your client to call you. Let him know when you will be calling.

Some people stop at this point, but you can go a few steps further. Ask your client if he would contact a certain number of referrals for you by sending a letter recommending your work. Make sure the letter states specifically what you have accomplished. Say, "I promise not to be upset if you want to use words like 'Great!' or 'Outstanding!'" This will get a chuckle and lets the client know what you want.

Some contacts might agree to send the letters on their own, and then provide you with the names and phone numbers with which to follow up. Sometimes you will have to send out the letters yourself. Keep a copy of these letters in your private portfolio to present to potential clients.

How many referrals should you ask for? Often one referral to a well-placed person is generous. On the other hand, Pastor has had as many as 30 referrals sent out on her behalf. It depends on how solid your relationship is with the client and how good a job you've done.

Pastor asks her client to send her a list of the people to whom the letters are sent before or as they are mailed. She follows up on the leads with a phone call within three days. Sometimes your client will say he cannot think of anybody in a decision-making position. Pastor once jokingly offered to review a client's Rolodex, and to her amazement he agreed! But you must have a very good rapport with your client plus chutzpah to pull this off.

5. *When you get a new client as a result of a referral, find a specific way of thanking your source.*

People want to help. They especially like knowing when they are successful. Therefore, let your client know when a recommendation she has made brings you new business. Find a special way to let her know how much you appreciate it. The process is simply not complete until you have said, "Thank you." Pastor has sent bouquets of flowers, concert tickets, or—in the case of an association executive who was fanatical about the game—an autographed baseball.

Upon meeting a new client, Pastor speaks positively about the person and the company that has provided the referral. On numerous occasions, she has been responsible for bringing the referring client and the new client together to do additional business.

P.J. Roach, who runs a real estate business in Boulder, Colorado, thanks those who successfully refer a client to him by paying for a dinner for two at a very fine restaurant. What's so unique about this? He chooses an exquisite restaurant at least one hour's drive from their home. It costs a bit, but it firmly plants P.J. in his client's memory.

"This way," he says, "they won't be able to use it right away because the distance requires them to plan for it." As the date approaches, they'll be talking about it and "probably also talk about me." They remember him, and when the couple runs into someone else who might need a real estate agent, who will they recommend?

How to Help Them Help You

It is unfortunate that far too many business and professional service providers never think of asking for referrals or, if they think of it, they are reluctant to ask because they feel it is inappropriate. Nothing is further from the truth.

I worked with a doctor who was intent on expanding his patient base but could not bring himself to ask existing patients to refer new ones. We got around the problem when I convinced him to post a pleasant sign in the waiting room that read: New Patient Referrals Cheerfully Accepted. In the weeks and months that followed, that simple sign prompted a number of his patients to comment to him, "You know, friends of mine just relocated in this area. I'll have them get in touch with you." A golden rule of leveraging your existing client and customer base is to let them know that you appreciate their referrals.

Joan Pastor conducted a survey of National Speakers Association members and received 285 responses. Twenty-one percent reported that their leads came from referrals three fourths of the time. Forty-three percent said they used testimonial letters to obtain referrals. They obtained letters from satisfied clients and customers that they reprinted and used in mailings and in presentations to prospective clients and customers.

Twenty-three percent of the respondents actually asked the referring party to send out the letter or make initial contact on their behalf! This may seem like a bold and aggressive strategy, yet those who are thoroughly satisfied with the job or service you have provided them don't see this as an inordinate task. In many cases, they are only too happy to do this.

What is the psychology behind asking them to go to bat on your behalf? The answer is they come off looking like a hero. Why? Whenever we make a wise purchase decision, we like to affirm our brilliance by sharing the discovery with others. The same holds true for those who use your services. Often, they are only too happy to let their friends and associates know about the crackerjack consultant/plumber/piano teacher/moving and storage company they had the foresight to hire.

While most people ask for referrals after a service has been provided, some professionals ask for referrals beforehand. How can one do this? The answer is to work the request into the conversation in a harmless way so that the client is willing to support you if you are willing to support him.

This is how I ask for referrals in advance of providing the service. First, I wait until the sale of my services is imminent. Then, when the client and I are at ease and discussing details, I casually say, "Now, of course, if I do a great job for you, I hope you will support me with a nice letter of recommendation." No one has ever objected to this. To the contrary, nearly all have supplied such a letter.

New Referral Incentives

Depending on the type of product or service you offer and the relationship with your existing customer or client base, you may find that by offering them one or more of the following, you can stimulate and increase the number of referrals you receive:

- ☐ Product or service discounts
- ☐ Product or service time extensions
- ☐ Free estimates, samples, or analyses
- ☐ Exclusive or charter memberships
- ☐ Quality or group discounts
- ☐ Extended warranties
- ☐ Additional products or services for no extra cost
- ☐ Extended telephone consultant privileges
- ☐ Extended or lifetime memberships
- ☐ Reduced costs on peripheral items or services
- ☐ Finder fees for new customers

One of my clients developed a program whereby whenever an existing customer recommended a new prospect who ultimately became a customer, the existing customer received a $500 bonus coupon towards purchases on his next order. In this case, each new customer represented several thousands of dollars worth of business to my client, and thus the $500 bonus coupon was in many respects a bargain. Some customers are eager to make referral "swaps." (More on this in later chapters.)

When offering any type of novelty item, particularly in the case of discounts or incentive programs, keep in mind what your cost would be to generate a new client or customer from scratch. When you weigh the costs of advertisements, sales representatives, printed literature, long-distance phone calls, meetings, and appointments against the cost of generating new business via an existing client incentive program, the incentive program wins hands down.

Incentive programs also help you sell more products more often to your existing customer base, and these are sales generated at far less overall marketing cost and effort.

MAKING YOUR CUSTOMERS LOOK GOOD

For an excellent continuing low-cost marketing strategy that works wonders, take time each week to make your customers look good.

Write letters of praise and nice notes to the people with whom you do business. Also write to their bosses, letting them know how much you enjoyed working with their employees and how valuable they were in assisting in the timely completion of your product or service delivery.

People do business with people they like. If you are functionally competent but take a cold and clinical approach to working with customers and clients, you are not practicing low-budget marketing at all. Rather, you are doing just the opposite. You are ensuring that you will have to generate dozens of new clients and customers to replace those who might otherwise give you additional business and offer good referrals. The goodwill that you build with your existing client base will be the most valuable asset that you could have.

A classic example of someone who took the time and effort to send nice notes to existing customers was Joe Girard. If he didn't make them look good, at least he made them feel good. Girard, who wrote the best-selling book *How to Sell Anything to Anybody* (New York: Simon & Schuster, 1977), established a comprehensive mailing system whereby each month he sent a "nice note" to all of his customers and prospects on his ever-growing mailing list.

After a while, this numbered in the thousands. Undaunted, Joe solicited the help of his family, helpers, and others. Each month, in a different size or different colored envelope so that no one would suspect what was coming, he kept in touch with everyone who had done business with him or was likely to do so. Did this strategy pay off? You bet! Joe is listed in the *Guinness Book of Records* as the all-time automobile sales record champion. In 1963, his first year, he sold 267 cars! Over the length of his career, he sold 13,000 cars.

Are there a few customers or clients to whom you should be sending cards? It doesn't cost that much (see Figure 3-1).

Novelty Items and Incentives

Depending on your product or service, one way to keep your company name at the forefront of your customers' minds is to supply them with useful novelty items. The best items are those which are continually visible, such as calendars, telephone decals,

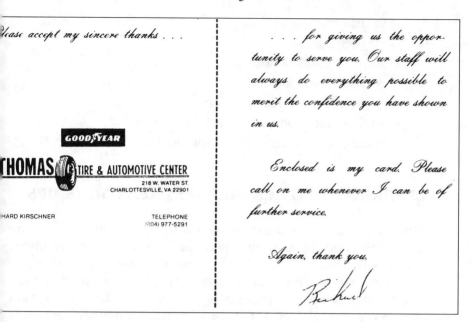

ease accept my sincere thanks . . .

GOODYEAR

THOMAS TIRE & AUTOMOTIVE CENTER
218 W. WATER ST
CHARLOTTESVILLE, VA 22901

HARD KIRSCHNER   TELEPHONE
(?04) 977-5291

*. . . for giving us the oppor-
tunity to serve you. Our staff will
always do everything possible to
merit the confidence you have shown
in us.*

*Enclosed is my card. Please
call on me whenever I can be of
further service.*

Again, thank you.

Figure 3-1. A thank-you card like this one is a fine good-will builder. Reprinted with permission.

key rings, and message holders. There is a wide variety of other items which also may be appropriate, depending on your business. These include:

- Road atlases
- Tote bags
- Pens, pencils, note pads
- Letter openers, desk sets
- Paper clip dispensers
- Business card cases
- Desk calendars, desk organizers, desk blotters
- Paper weights, door stops
- Clocks, calculators
- Luggage tags
- Clip boards, bulletin boards
- Drinking cup insulators

☐ Yardsticks, rulers

☐ Magnets, decals

☐ Software holders, folders

☐ Preprinted Rolodex cards

☐ Business card holders, folders

☐ Wall plaque mottos, desk plaque mottos

☐ Photograph pictures, autograph books

LEVERAGING OTHER BUSINESS RELATIONSHIPS

While we're on the topic of using leverage to enhance shoestring marketing efforts, you should periodically call former customers. Every company, no matter how big or little, has lost some customers. At one time, these individuals were convinced enough to buy your company's product or service. Then for some reason they became displeased (or were attracted to another company) and never returned.

Getting these people interested in your company again is a worthwhile goal for several reasons. First, while you're discovering what made them ex-customers or ex-clients, you'll be conducting valuable research into how your company works and how it is perceived. Second, the word-of-mouth praise from a customer you have won back is likely to be more effusive than from one who has been satisfied all along.

Even in the case where previous customers left disgruntled or displeased, time often heals all, and three or six months later they may again be willing to talk and, in fact, do business with you.

For two years I took my car to the Cross Roads Amoco station because they repaired it without charging a fortune. Early one winter evening, after having left my car there for the day to be repaired, it conked out as I was driving away from the station. To my dismay it would not start, and worse, this was not the problem for which I had brought my car to the station in the first place.

As fate would have it, the attendant on duty could not start the car. I insisted that because I had brought my car there for repair without the problem of it shorting out, it was the station's responsibility to start me and send me on my way. After about 30 minutes, I hailed a fellow customer who was able to start my car. Upset with the performance of the station attendant, I decided never to go back to that station.

One day in a parking garage, I passed the owner of the station who cheerfully commented, "Well, we haven't seen you in a while. Why don't you bring your car in for your next tune-up?" His request prompted me to do just that. Time had passed and my disappointment with his station attendant seemed like a small issue.

To regain a customer, it's important to discover the source of displeasure. Telephoning or asking in person will bring you the best results, far better than sending a letter or questionnaire. The most vital elements are humility and sincerity. Explain that you would like to know why they are no longer customers, and apologize for any trouble your company may have caused. Thank the person for his or her time, saying that you will rectify the situation.

If the person has a valid complaint, ethically you must replace the defective equipment or correct any damage caused by improper service performed by your company. Encourage customers to believe you are adding an extra touch and individual attention. If the person is complaining about matters beyond your control, sympathize and say goodbye. That person is not likely to return as a customer.

Calling on former customers allows you to pinpoint the source of problems and remedy them before other customers complain. Handled correctly, you will have a satisfied customer who will praise your efforts to remedy the problem.

Leveraging Other Resources

Another way to use leverage is to "lean" on your suppliers. Their suggestions for gaining additional business, as well as providing specific leads, could make your day.

Always solicit suggestions from your employees. If your employees do not have responsibility for marketing, they still meet and encounter others who may have need of your products and services (see Chapter 4). Marketing should be a company-wide effort, and in the broader sense marketing should be everyone's responsibility. From the top salesperson to the receptionist, every member of your staff is important to the marketing team. Moreover, any new business efforts you undertake may not improve the long-term viability of your company if your staff is not helpful and informed.

IN-HOUSE MARKETING ASSESSMENT

In addition to leveraging your existing customer or client base, it is also essential that you make some basic in-house assessments. Which marketing strategies and vehicles generate the greatest number of new clients? Which generate high-volume clients?

To undertake this analysis, simply list on a piece of paper or a software spreadsheet all the vehicles you presently employ regardless of cost. This could include: marketing at trade shows; distributing printed advertisements like flyers, handbills, and posters; cultivating customer referrals; getting articles published; generating speaking engagements; arranging store front displays, and so forth (see table below).

In a second column, indicate the number of new clients or customers you have gained in the past year via the various mar-

Assessment of Marketing Vehicles (Hypothetical)

Vehicle	Number of Customers	Amount of Revenue	Revenue Per Customer
Flyers	3	$ 840	$280
Handbills	8	1,250	156
Posters	1	300	300
Customer Referrals	4	3,500	875
Articles	6	2,880	480
Speaking engagements	5	2,750	550
Store front displays	1	700	700
Yellow Pages ads	5	2,600	520
Sending out brochures	2	1,200	600
Direct mail	7	1,000	143
Professional meetings	4	$1,800	$450

keting strategies and vehicles, and in a third column, list the total amount of revenue.

You can quickly determine which marketing vehicles have been most effective for you in terms of generating sheer numbers of new customers (column 2), and which were most effective in terms of generating the largest average dollar value per new customer (column 4). For most businesses with whom I have worked, referrals show up best when this type of analysis is undertaken. However, it is useful for your own purpose to know exactly which vehicle has worked best for you in the past so you will know where to focus your efforts in the future.

You can also sum the marketing costs of the various strategies and vehicles, i.e., those items in column 1, and devise a revenue/cost ratio. It will take some executive decisions to properly allocate marketing costs among the various vehicles since some costs are shared and not otherwise easily allocated. However, if you undertake this analysis even in crude measure, you will gain excellent in-house marketing vehicle assessment information.

Using customer leverage strategies to generate additional and new business should always be first on your list of low-cost but highly effective marketing vehicles.

4

MARKETING THROUGH THE TELEPHONE

Words are finite organs of the infinite mind.

Ralph Waldo Emerson

The telephone, invented by Alexander Graham Bell in 1876, has been in widespread use throughout the United States since the early part of this century. The use of telephones in business has prompted a steady stream of improvements. In the last 10 years, the rate of technological enhancement has grown at an exponential rate. One would think that after all this time businesses would have mastered the use of the telephone by strengthening the weakest link in the communication network—humans—through proper training. Unfortunately, this is not so.

Studies reveal that telephone business usage, particularly reception, remains poor. One research group called more than 5000 Yellow Page advertisers to say, "I saw your ad in the Yellow Pages. How much does your product (or service) cost?" The response statistics were outrageous. Over 78% never asked for the caller's name. Over 55% took more than eight rings to answer. Over 42% gave the price, then listed other products and services without gauging the caller's interest. Other atrocities revealed in this experiment are reflected in these responses:

- ☐ "We don't advertise in the Yellow Pages"
- ☐ "I don't know. Can you call back when the boss is here?"

Many spoke so rapidly that it was difficult to determine the name of the company or division. Lack of enthusiasm or empathy also were evident in many responses. Less than 10% answered the phone in a courteous professional manner or made the callers feel that their business was desired.

DEGENERATING CAPABILITIES

Why has proper use of the telephone, particularly in business, degenerated over the years? The answer must lie in the top management's regard for its use. For example, who is hired to answer the phone? Individuals with the aptitude and learning capability to do a good job in this area? Or is it simply the least expensive body that could be plunked down in front of the phone?

As owner or manager, have you taken the time to develop a phone reception system—a consistent manner in which employees of your company answer the phone, page others, take messages, and treat callers? I doubt if there is a specific formula that works for all organizations in all situations. Depending on the nature of your business, it may be necessary to screen heavily for executives or support staff. If you have not established a system, then you are losing out in one of the least expensive, most important aspects of shoestring marketing.

Your telephone system is expensive, even if you have the simplest of systems and only one line. The people who call your company inquiring about your products or services are the single most valuable commodity in the long-term prosperity of your enterprise. Until you recognize this, and become 100% telephone responsive—"give good phone"—you are pouring marketing leads down the drain. Worse, you are shortchanging the effectiveness of your entire marketing program.

WORLD CLASS TELEPHONE RECEPTION

What are the hallmarks of a company that knows how to answer the telephone and how to treat those who call? Try these on for size:

Strive to answer the phone on the second or third ring and certainly no later than the fourth ring.   If necessary, realign your staff or your office so that this can be accomplished. Even under a restricted budget, you can't afford to convey the image of a company that doesn't care about its callers. This is exactly the message you offer when your phones are answered on the fifth ring, sixth ring or later.

Slowly and clearly answer by stating the company name. You and I have made a hundred calls that have been answered by people responding so quickly and automatically that it is literally impossible to determine what they have said upon answering the phone. I often take it upon myself to try to correct this situation for other companies by saying, "I am sorry, I didn't catch a word of that." How will your potential customers feel if, when greeted, they can't catch a word of what your telephone receptionists are saying?

Smile into the phone.   People report that they can literally hear a smile. Veteran telephone sales trainers advise placing a mirror next to your phone so that you can continually observe yourself while speaking. I find that my blank computer screen does just as well. If you or your employees who answer the phone are constantly in a rush, put this book down right now and consider the consequences of sending that message over the telephone line. Would you want to do business with you?

The strict rules of customer service apply over the phone. Review the list presented at the end of Chapter 2 on customer service. These rules are as important to follow over the phone as they are when encountering people in person. Displaying enthusiasm, friendliness, and courtesy over the phone are not platitudes; the life blood of your business is on the line.

Consider the rate at which our society has come to rely upon phones. As more women enter the workforce, phone orders for goods and services necessarily increase. Before the early 1970s, the traditional American family of 2.4 children was blessed with a full-time housekeeper, errand runner, and shopper—the housewife. Now, families as well as single professionals are relying more on time-saving devices to take care of their needs. Hence, almost irrespective of what you offer, the importance of the telephone caller to the success of your business will increase.

The Opportunity in Every Inquiry

Since your employees are public contact points for any marketing campaign, they must be trained to recognize the opportunity in every telephone inquiry. Convey to them that their contact with customers and prospective customers far outweighs the best advertising and promotion plan that you may be undertaking. Avoid having the newest and least informed person inherit the counter work or telephone reception responsibilities. There is a natural tendency for businesses to do this, but the frontline duty should go to someone who is equipped to handle the job.

Next, recognize that you set the example. If you are patient, understanding and interested in the questions posed to you when answering the phone, then your staff is likely to treat customers in the same manner. A key to ensuring that your staff answers the phone properly is to provide them with a list of typical questions asked by customers and the answers to those questions. Also provide them with a small organizational or departmental chart listing the roles and responsibilities of other employees.

You need to keep your staff informed, and this takes work. If you are the elusive executive, and your telephone receptionist(s) is constantly forced to tell people, "He is busy right now," "She is not available, may I take a message?" or "He is out of the office," then your system is not very effective.

Robert Townsend in *Up the Organization* (New York: Ballantine, 1978) advises that if you want to gain a real sense of what indignities your defenses inflict on callers, call your company in a disguised voice and ask for yourself. Also, periodically throughout the day have associates call your company, pose different questions to whomever answers, and carefully jot down responses. This eye-opening exercise will reveal room for improvement.

Tell your staff which types of calls should get through and which ones shouldn't. If you must resort to heavy screening, make sure that your receptionist offers the utmost in courtesy. The question, "What is it you need to speak to him about?" steps on the privacy of the caller and possibly the caller's feelings. There are many other ways to convey to callers that you are not available right now and capture the essence of why they are calling.

Consider having your telephone receptionist offer such messages as:

☐ "Ms. X has a full schedule today but would be pleased to return your call on Thursday morning. May I give her a message?"

☐ "Mr. Z will be attending meetings today until late afternoon, but he has asked me to get complete messages so he can get back to you as quickly as possible."

Yes, these are long and involved passages, but they convey courtesy, understanding, and a sense of the caller's importance.

Convince your employees that they are part of an overall marketing team. One company initiated a month long program to remind employees of the importance of providing effective telephone response to the company's marketing program. Employees were given buttons that read "It *is* my job." They were also asked to submit a list of five questions most commonly asked by callers along with suggested responses. Then, at a company-wide meeting these questions were discussed and the 10 most frequently asked questions and responses were printed and distributed to everyone.

Also stress the importance of taking messages for one another. Create an atmosphere in which kudos are offered for those who go out of their way to answer a co-worker's telephone or the telephone that is ringing after hours. As the messages taken for one another improve, staff response to all incoming calls will improve as well. If your staff is large enough and the atmosphere is conducive, establish a "message taker" of the week or month award. Yes, it really is this important to instill sound phone reception techniques among your staff.

Putting Customers on Hold

Ideally, you never want to put a customer on hold because you introduce the possibility that he will hang up. However, placing customers on hold is a business fact of life in many operations. It would be far too costly to have a receptionist available every moment someone calls.

If you must place callers on hold, here are a few simple rules:

☐ Always have receptionists ask, "May I put you on hold?" and then give the caller time to respond. Many callers, particularly those calling long distance, do not wish to be placed on hold, and with good reason. This is not to say that long-distance callers get priority over local callers. Consider, however, that for whatever the reason, the long-distance caller may have greater motivation to get in touch with you because he is paying for the call.

☐ Avoid irritating jingles, music and repeating messages. Many callers, who are prepared to wait, continue working at their desks and appreciate the lack of noise, while waiting for a human being to return to the line.

☐ Automated, one-time messages are acceptable. Your message could ask the caller not to hang up, state that the call will be answered in turn, warn that this is a very busy period of the day, etc. Your message could also conclude with a brief description of your products or services. Many businesses find that additional sales are generated because of this extra message. Callers seeking information on one product may learn about another product while on hold.

☐ When your receptionist actually comes on the line, make sure that all of the recommendations offered for proper telephone reception throughout this chapter are followed. If your receptionist answers in a rush as if this call were unimportant and there were dozens more waiting, your company's overall marketing efforts will suffer.

DOUBLING YOUR PHONE PRODUCTIVITY THROUGH HEADSETS

Whether you manage a company of one or 100, simple inexpensive technology is available immediately to double your telephone usage efficiency.

Businesses that make or receive more than a few phone calls a day are fortunate to have a wide selection of supporting equipment. The "old style" phone is familiar to most of us. Many people try to balance the receiver between the ear and shoulder while taking notes or leafing through files. Sometimes it drops on the desk. Sometimes it disconnects the caller as the receiver cradle gets nudged when we reach for a paper across the desk.

One of the best ways to alleviate such problems and attain greater efficiency and convenience is to use a telephone headset. Headsets are not just for telephone operators. They are for executives, too. They are provided by a variety of communications and telephone equipment companies and generally comprise a set of lightweight earphones with a long prong bending toward the mouth. This ear and mouthpiece set is attached by a cord to a desktop dialing module.

The first thing you will notice about the telephone headset is the *mobility* it provides. When you wear one, your hands are free to take notes, juggle papers, or open file drawers. Yet, they have a sound quality equal to the traditional handset phone, and infinitely superior to the speaker phones that rely on amplification of your voice. If your company does any telemarketing, headsets are essential for those individuals since they often need to write or type orders while on the phone.

One expert observed that "Lightweight headsets offer hands free communication aimed at the heavy telephone user. Telemarketers, telephone sales representatives, reservation agents, customer service representatives, and computer operators represent the range of business applications that require hands-free operation." It is my belief that if you spend even 30 minutes per day on the phone, headsets are a sound investment.

Another advantage cited by headset users is *less fatigue.* If you make and receive several phone calls, one of the most efficient ways to handle them is to reserve a specific block of time—say, two hours in the afternoon—to return and generate calls. This alleviates the problem of the phone as a constant interruption of other work. However, you quickly find out that an hour or more on the phone is tiring. A telephone headset alleviates this. I've used them for four years. 10 to 15 calls used to be drudgery. Now I mow them down without fatigue! You can move around a bit, stretch your neck and back, and generally combat the tiring feeling of sitting in one spot for hours on end.

Telephone headset manufacturers are constantly seeking ways to add greater comfort. Headsets have now evolved from large, heavy "earmuff" equipment to extremely lightweight pieces contoured for comfortable ear fit.

Increased efficiency is another valuable benefit cited by headset users. If it takes you as much as two hours to make ten calls, you are likely to be able to improve on that statistic with a headset. There are a variety of reasons for this greater efficiency, not the least of which is that you can do other productive work while you're on hold. Additionally, you'll find you can respond to questions much faster when your hands are free to look through the files for answers. And, when the task of making phone calls is more comfortable, you don't give in to the temptation to waste time between calls.

Another advantage of headsets is their ability to cut out *distractions.* While you are wearing earphones, you simply don't have the background noise typical of handset phones. You don't hear phones ring in the next office, and you aren't tempted to carry on two conversations at once—one with your secretary in the next office and one with the individual on the other end of the phone.

The cost of a headset is relatively low, starting at $39.95, and since there are many competitors in the market, you can shop around. All headsets are not equal. Some are specially designed for high noise environments, with earphones that insulate you from outside noise particularly well. Warranties and service policies will also vary.

MAKING SURE CALLERS CAN REACH YOU

If you move outside of your local area, you can have your telephone number changed and the telephone company will provide a recording giving callers the new number. As long as this recording is provided, it is a pretty safe bet that callers will use the new number and contact you. The phone company offers this as a free service, usually for up to one year. However, the phone company will not guarantee how long the recording will remain in place. So, if you have moved, periodically call your old number to see what message, if any, callers are getting. If callers are getting the message that "this number has been disconnected," call the phone company immediately to see what type of arrangement can be made to either reissue the message offering the new number or discuss other options. The term "disconnected" implies to many people that the company went out of business. You can't afford this implication.

You may also choose to keep your old telephone number and pay an additional monthly service charge based on the distance from your original area. Procedures and fees vary, so check with your the local telephone company.

To ensure that you don't miss any calls after leaving an area, you could retain your old phone number indefinitely and have an answering service or machine capture all calls. This introduces added expense, but how important is each lost call to you? You could use the telephone company's free message, for up to a year, and then evaluate the necessity of monitoring your old phone line.

THE TELEPHONE AS A PROACTIVE SALES TOOL

Thus far we have discussed incoming calls and their effect on marketing. Obviously, the telephone can be used when prospecting for new business. If you don't have a large bank of telephones used to make sales pitches to a large list of potential customers, you may think your business isn't involved in telemarketing. Think again. You and others in your organization are involved in telemarketing every time you find yourself on the phone explaining your products or services, answering the questions of customers, or convincing clients to buy.

You may make cold calls through a specific, concentrated effort or you may merely respond to inquiries. It is all marketing by telephone.

There are several excellent texts available that cover telemarketing, and even if your mode of generating new business does not involve telemarketing, I recommend that you review at least one of the following:

☐ *How to Make Appointments by Telephone,* by Mona Ling (Englewood Cliffs, NJ: Prentice-Hall, 1963)

☐ *Getting New Clients,* by R. Connor and J. Davidson (New York: Wiley, 1987)

☐ *The Soft Sell,* by Tim Connor (Crofton, MD: T.R. Training Associates, 1981)

Telemarketing Offers Shoestring Firepower

Because you already have telephones installed, their use for marketing is one of the least expensive ways of reaching potential customers. With the increasing "high tech" orientation of business, the "high touch" of human voice communication is one of today's effective marketing strategies. The more we encounter machines, the more impressed we are by a personal deviation from them. A phone call provides that deviation.

Unfortunately, the average person—even the entrepreneur who has the fortitude to start his/her own business—feels awkward and even fearful about using the telephone for marketing purposes. We simply don't know how to use the phone. We don't know how to open the conversation, how to pursue it to its logical conclusion or how to close it gracefully. We shrink from the cold call that pits us against a person who might hang up on us. We also avoid calls to previous customers or to prospects because we fear that they might be inconvenienced.

Being Yourself

The best way to approach telephone marketing is also the easiest: Just be yourself. That means sounding human rather than mechanical, and it starts with your opening statement. For example, you might be tempted to say something stiff, because you feel stiff—something like, "Good morning, Mrs. Jones. I hope you'll give me a minute of your time to tell you about. . . . " But that's not how you normally speak. A better approach is your own more normal pattern of speech, probably more like: "Hi, How are ya? I'm calling to see if. . . . "

Jot down notes of what you want to cover in a phone call, but resist the temptation to follow a canned speech. It will sound exactly like what it is—something you are reading. That makes it very easy for the person on the other end of the line to hang up. It is much more difficult to hang up on someone who comes across as being human.

Many successful entrepreneurs occasionally "do phone" as a way of practicing their skills and keeping in touch with how customers and potential customers feel about their products. The more calls you make, especially if you remember to be yourself, the better you become. Telemarketing experience will have a favorable spillover effect in terms of how you respond to phone inquiries and how you approach people who already are clients.

Whom to Call

Initially, your calls to previous customers or clients to inform them of a new product or service are likely to be your most successful. You already have a track record with these companies and individuals, so you can assume that they will have some interest in listening to you. Hereafter, any time you have news that may interest a client, from expansion of your product line to new staff members or equipment, by all means use telephone marketing.

Developing a specific campaign, such as a "one day sale for our preferred customers only," can work particularly well with established customers.

Start making cold calls (my friend Dennis Fox calls them "warm calls") to companies and individuals who have never used your products or services. You will need to be selective. Identify the most likely new clients by their lines of work, their neighborhoods, their pastimes, the ages of their children or other features that relate to your marketing needs (see Chapter 1). Just start. Leave your fears behind.

What to Say

In addition to developing an appropriate conversational style and identifying targets to call, there is still the question of content. This largely depends on what you are marketing. Elements that most telemarketing contacts should cover include:

- *Introduction*—"Hi, I'm_____, with_____company."
- *Credibility statement*—Especially for cold calls, a statement that quickly establishes your business credibility.
- *Reminder statement*—When calling previous customers, you may need to remind them that they have done business with you in the past.
- *Interest generating statement*—A mention of new products, new prices, new capabilities or other attention-getting highlights.
- *Product/service statement*—A brief description of what you can offer.
- *Probing discussion*—If possible, learn more about the potential customers' needs, reasonable potential, etc.

Prepare for notetaking when you are making telemarketing calls. Establish a log of contacts, dates called, and their responses. This log helps you develop a strategy for calling back later. You may not close sales or get appointments on a first call, but with patience and practice you'll find that telemarketing can have a valuable payoff.

5

USING PART-TIME HELP

Money still talks, but nowadays it has to catch its breath more often.

Anonymous

At speaking engagements and in private consulting over the years, I have been amazed by the number of independent entrepreneurs who employ numerous full-time employees, yet are reluctant to use part-time help.

Let's examine some marketing related uses for part-time help. How many of the following tasks have you assigned to full-time, (and probably expensive) employees, and how many are consuming your own precious time?

- ☐ answering requests for information
- ☐ sending out advertisements/mailings of any sort
- ☐ serving routine customer needs
- ☐ routing/sorting mail
- ☐ making deliveries/pick-ups
- ☐ researching/surveying customers and their needs
- ☐ keeping track of necessary trade publications and news sources
- ☐ typing mailing lists

- typing anything, for that matter
- answering the phone/routing calls
- cleaning, repairing
- studying the competition, their literature, and products
- first round/lead calling
- hunting for a product or service you need
- cataloging new information or products
- proofreading copy for marketing literature, memos, letters
- tracking or arranging inventory or displays
- doing anything that a less essential part-time employee could do without excessive guidance

If you're like most other small business owners or managers, you're doing too many of these tasks or delegating them to full-time employees. "Someone has to stick mailing labels on the envelopes and keep track of inventory or competitor information, but I just don't have the money to hire a clerk." If you don't have the funds or the need for a *full-time* clerical assistant, then part-time help is the answer. Firms accrue many benefits from using part-timers. Three major advantages are:

- **Flexibility**. Part-timers are available to adjust your production to meet market demand and they are usually easy to acquire and to release as necessary.
- **Low cost**. Part-timers not only work for less than their full-time counterparts, they also receive few of the expensive benefits full-timers receive, particularly medical insurance and paid vacations.
- **High productivity**. Recent surveys dispute the myth that part-timers are generally less productive than full-timers, and in fact, due to the concentrated nature of their work and less taxing work schedules, some managers find that part-timers are more productive per dollar.

There are several types of part-timers. Some may be more suitable to your needs than others. These include permanent part-time employees, temporaries, students (high school, college, and grad school), retirees, foreign exchange students, college interns, and even your employees' own kids or spouses.

It is very likely that you can find a bright, motivated student out there to help with your business. The schools are full of intelligent, perceptive young men and women, many of whom are just waiting for an opportunity to gain experience. Just because they are part-time help doesn't mean they're less intelligent or effective. Many can take a "divisible" unit of work and do a bang-up job on it.

FIVE DOLLARS AN HOUR STILL BUYS A LOT

I questioned busy entrepreneurs who were trying to accomplish many marketing tasks on their own. I found that the reason they chose not to use part-time help was that they felt they simply could not afford it. Yet, every community has hundreds of bright, high school juniors and seniors who are thrilled at the possibility of working for $5.00 an hour—an amount well above the minimum wage. This may not seem like a lot of money to you, but to them it may be, especially when combined with hands-on experience in their chosen field.

In this era of entrepreneurism, there is a strong desire among youth to be successful in business and in a career. The time has never been better for small to medium sized business entrepreneurs to benefit from using high school and college students.

For example, I employ one or two students throughout the year on a part-time basis after school, occasionally on weekends and during school holidays. The 8 to 12 hours per week that my part-timers average is invaluable to me. I never miss the $40 to $60 per week that I pay them. I have used part-time students to:

☐ stuff envelopes for direct mail campaigns
☐ do marketing research over the phone or at the local library
☐ proofread items that clients will be seeing
☐ take business photos of me
☐ design a new logo

☐ help me think through my marketing strategy

☐ work on my computer

Some of the students I have employed are just as effective and productive as the $25,000 or $30,000 per year employees whom I supervised before venturing out on my own. They are a lot cheaper and easier to hire.

Inexpensive Word Processing Help

There is a nationwide force of highly efficient word processors who operate out of their own homes. These word processors are usually women raising small children and seeking to generate additional income for their families. Having little or no overhead, yet remaining competitive, these word processors charge 20% to 50% less than word processing companies.

The beauty of working with a home-based word processor is that you do not have to keep them fully occupied. You only pay for the services that you need. With the variety of word processing software programs and a vast array of print options, your part-time word processor can offer a real boost to your marketing efforts if your business involves preparing bids, proposals, sales letters, capability statements, or other written marketing tools.

GETTING OVER THE HIRING HURDLE

What are some other reasons many small entrepreneurs don't hire part-time help? Often they believe that:

☐ the part-timer won't be as loyal as other employees

☐ they won't have the same measure of control over part-timers as they have over full-time staff

☐ they will waste a lot of time teaching and supervising someone who will be on the job a few hours a week for a few months

☐ a part-timer's references will probably be less comprehensive and exact than a regular employee's

Most employers want employees who won't cause problems. They want people who come in punctually every day, get started easily, take directions, do the job, and rarely get sick, complain, or ask for a raise. There is a myth among entrepreneurs that part-time employees won't fit in or will require extensive training or hand-holding to do the simplest work.

Granted, there are some types of work you cannot quickly delegate to a part-timer. However, many tasks are easily handled by someone with a minimum of training—probably many of the tasks you are performing now. The important first step is to identify these tasks.

What to Assign

Part-time workers should be assigned easily defined activities with clear starting and finishing points, tasks that don't require excessive supervision. One way to begin using part-timers is to assign them what I call seed work—all those useful yet bothersome tasks that you have been putting off:

- □ running errands around town
- □ making early-round phone calls
- □ visiting competitors' stores (if you're in retailing)
- □ studying competitors' literature
- □ using competitors' products/services
- □ surveying customers
- □ making library research trips
- □ compiling data on your own products or services

Seed work should be a very distinct unit of work. For example, let's say you want information on the eight other companies in your line of business within a 10-mile radius. A high school student can easily visit the sites, write for the brochures (using his/her home address), and summarize the information gathered. A more experienced employee could spot trends or innovations from this data, all with a minimum of your time spent on instruction. "But my company requires information that not just any Joe Schmoe could compile. What I need takes some skill and intelligence. That's why I do it myself." True, sometimes portions of the work must be completed by a seasoned expert—but only portions.

Part-time employees can help you make exploratory phone calls to identify the proper name and direct dial phone number of high quality prospects, whom you then call. The part-timer can also undertake marketing research at the library, gathering key articles, names and information, directories, and new product information. They can be used in the area of customer follow-up, calling to confirm that customers received their shipments on time. Part-timers can also help out with recordkeeping and clerical duties.

When Business Isn't Booming

If business is not going well, and you have been working with a number of part-time employees, it is much easier to reduce staff or redirect efforts than when you are working with full-time employees. Part-timers, recognizing that they are the "last hired and first to go" are more agreeable to a reduction in hours, a change in assignments, and general shifting of priorities.

The odd jobs that you might have local high school students do—such as filing, sending out advertising, washing the trucks—could be cut back during lean times. If necessary, your full-time employees could devote more of their time and efforts to generating new business, while part-timers handle the full-timers' routine or mundane responsibilities. Their flexibility and relative low rate of pay might be part of the formula that gets you through a crunch time until revenues start to increase.

When Business Is Stable or Increasing

The hallmark of a successful entrepreneur and an effective shoe-string marketer is his ability to look beyond the current level of adequacy and plan for the future of the enterprise. Whether your business is doing well right now or is just starting to take off, part-timers can play an important role in your success. If your full-time staff is working overtime just to fill orders, you will soon realize that overtime pay is an expensive proposition. Part-timers could be the answer.

During boom time, it helps to have somebody to straighten out the product literature rack, answer the increased number of customer inquiries, and keep the store or shop in top shape. Too many entrepreneurs find themselves performing these and other clerical duties to save a dollar. Their resources would be better directed towards more important priorities.

You never want to reach the point where your shoestring marketing efforts cause you to race around the clock. If you do, you will fail to recognize the value of your ability to think clearly in directing overall marketing efforts.

During boom time, your staff needs a break too. Even the most highly productive and happy employees can quickly reach their tolerance level. Too many entrepreneurs recognize these changes, but cannot bring themselves to bring in the part-timers who are so sorely needed. If you get so busy that you don't even have the time to regroup and hire part-timers, then you're simply too busy.

Maintaining Your File

I recommend maintaining a file of local students, temporaries, and retirees who have the skills you need and can be summoned on fairly short notice. During boom time, one part-time employee could call from this file and set up appointments to hire another. You wouldn't even have to waste the time calling and arranging interviews. A successful business should have the flexibility to handle the up and down periods before they occur. It behooves you to experiment with part-time help, whether you need it or not, just to see the potential benefit.

One of my clients, a highly capable personal computer consultant, has operated for five years without any part-time help. Although he frequently calls me to say he is (1) swamped, (2) taking on some assignments that are not really worth his time, and (3) unable to really sit down and plan things, he repeatedly has ignored my recommendation that he hire some part-time helpers. The Promethean urge within us to be self-sufficient becomes foolhardy in the context of operating one's own venture, particularly among independent entrepreneurs.

The Paperwork Game

In 1975, when I worked at Burroughs Business Machines, now called Unisys, we had a product literature rack with 20 or so different specification sheets. Everyone would go grab what they needed, and inevitably the literature rack was a disaster area. The boss would not allow anyone to spend his or her valuable time straightening it out. An economical policy, you think? Not at all. Whenever we needed a flyer, we had to spend considerable time hunting through the paper jungle to find what we needed. Not only did this waste our time, but expensive spec sheets got lost or mangled in the process. This job (and many others around the office) would have been ideal for a part-time student from the local high school.

Before working for me, one of my research assistants and a part-time employee, Louis Baron, managed a 30,000 document software documentation library for a business software corporation. He received the ID number of all newly created or updated software documentation, printed out a copy, and filed it in one of the archival books. This work supported more than 50 computer programmers. When one of the programmers wanted a hard copy from the files, Louis retrieved it and checked it out to them. When they returned it, he checked it back in. Furthermore, he updated three different indexes so the programmers could find what they needed quickly, and he kept back-up copies of the documentation in a file cabinet full of disks.

Before Louis was hired, the programmers had to do all this work themselves. Needless to say, with 50 users and no one responsible for keeping the place organized, it was a real mess. One of the programmers' supervisors frequently had to take time out from her busy schedule to try to keep the place uncluttered. It didn't work. What a waste!

Once properly organized, the documentation library took less time and effort to maintain. With his free time, Louis then ran errands, covered the telephones for the secretaries when they were out, looked up codes and information for the programmers, and did whatever anyone needed done. All this for $5.75 an hour and very little training required. Could your business use a part-timer like Louis?

Dialing for Dollars

Who does the phoning in your office or firm? In Chapter 4 we discussed the importance of the telephone in almost any business venture. Whether it's handling routine calls, information dispersal, information gathering, or customer surveys, someone has to be on your end of the receiver. Here are some of the things a good part-timer can do with a phone to aid in your marketing efforts:

☐ Answer and route incoming calls, take messages

☐ Respond to telephone requests for information

☐ Research/hunt down information for you—for instance, finding names, direct lines, addresses, best prices, most convenient locations

☐ Call customers for an after-the-sale satisfaction check. This is an excellent way to learn about your product's performance

☐ Survey by telephone

☐ Sell a specific product, service, or special offer

☐ *Anything* that alleviates you or your employees of having to make more than one call to achieve desired results.

Before you begin, you must give the part-timer some background information on what they will be seeking, selling, or researching. Nothing destroys a customer's confidence more than getting a blank answer to a crucial question. Finally, and most important, give the caller a basic script or Q & A sheet, but make it clear that it should not be read verbatim. A little enthusiasm can go a long way in making a pitch sound interesting. You could have your telemarketer hunt only for potential interest and have a full time professional call back later.

HOW AND WHERE TO FIND PART-TIMERS

At first, finding part-timers may seem difficult, but you'll learn quickly. Don't look in the *New York Times*. The people you're seeking may not be formally searching for a job. You may have to use alternative ways to find them.

The fastest way to locate high school students is to call the high schools within a five-mile radius of your location and ask to speak to the guidance counselor or job placement counselor. For college or graduate students, call the universities within your metro area and ask for the career placement office. A college student usually can drive a greater distance to work than a high school student. Most high schools, community colleges, and universities have job bank coordinators who list part-time and summer jobs on their bulletin boards.

The job bank coordinator will ask:

☐ How many hours per week do you need help?
☐ Where are you located? Is a car necessary?
☐ What is the rate of pay?
☐ What type of business are you in?
☐ What kind of work will the student be doing?
☐ What particular skills or experience will the students need?

For some college students, especially graduate students, the placement office may want more specific information about the job requirements. Also, don't neglect the high school and college newspapers. They may attract more responses than the coordinator's bulletin board.

Finding word processing help and other contracted skilled laborers requires a little more effort but is well worth the time. Home-based word processors, for example, are apt to advertise in the Yellow Pages with a simple one-line listing, beside larger ads indicating business district locations, placed by word processing support companies.

Bulletin boards located in community institutions are a good place to advertise for the services you seek. These include libraries, supermarkets, and school bulletin boards. "Job Wanted" ads also may be posted. State and county job banks are good sources for part-time employees, especially employees with some specific blue-collar experience to their credit.

Local newspapers (and some community shopper guides) are particularly good for placing a part-time job notice. These papers are inexpensive and aimed at a specific town or neighborhood.

They allow exposure to people at home, housewives, retirees, and students.

Association Help

The Association of Part-Time Professionals is a good source of skilled professional workers. The APTP offers prospective employers a job referral service, a network of part-time job contacts, a quarterly newsletter including an employment classified section, and the APTP Employer Directory, which lists employers of part-time professionals.

The association membership includes retirees, women re-entering the workforce, disabled individuals, and graduate students. For more information, contact APTP, 7655 Old Springhouse Road, McLean, VA 22102, (703) 734-7975.

Opposites May Attract, But . . .

For clerical support and marketing research, the part-timer should be somewhat like you. If the employees are expected to make responsible choices, they must understand what you want to accomplish. Anyone who does not fully understand your mission may act as a passive or unconscious resister.

INTERNSHIPS

Imagine this scenario: You hire an undergraduate or graduate marketing whiz kid looking for experience and useful knowledge. Further, this assistant receives academic credit for his or her work. Hence, the student is motivated. Perhaps you even have several marketing students working for you. What could you expect?

John T. McCarrier, manager of marketing research at Toledo Scale in Worthington, Ohio, learned about internship programs during a difficult time. A hiring freeze collided with his need for additional help. The temporary solution of hiring several students from the marketing department at Ohio State University for part-time work has become a permanent and valuable practice.

McCarrier is convinced that this program is mutually rewarding and says he would recommend it wholeheartedly to other market research managers.

"A market research department is an excellent place to use student help," says McCarrier. Much of the work is organized into discrete projects that can be scheduled with varying levels of effort during the students' term to match hours available. This contrasts with many departments that must produce consistent results daily.

"Working on projects," McCarrier says, "also gives students fast feedback and a feeling of being responsible for an identifiable result." While their school can give them an effective education in marketing, nothing can substitute for actual experience.

The variety of work carried out by the marketing department continually challenges students. "Also, students bring a freshness to their jobs that more than compensates for their initial inexperience," says McCarrier. "Their enthusiasm makes them good telephone interviewers and carries them through routine chores."

"The market research department interacts with almost all other departments of the company," McCarrier adds. "This allows a look at the other divisions and their interactions with one another." Within the market research department, in addition to routine duties, each intern is given responsibility for one area that the department serves: retail products, standard industrial products, and scale systems used in manufacturing facilities. "This system gives interns a feeling of belonging to a team, as well as making them more knowledgeable and effective in their assigned product areas," says McCarrier.

Running Your Own Internship Program

McCarrier offers a few tips for running an internship program:

- ☐ If you will be using many interns, it will be easier to find a single school to supply you with students. Keeping track of only one set of exam and vacation schedules will be much easier than working around a multitude of dates.
- ☐ Find out about the kind of experiences the schools will qualify as internships. The rules differ. (This is a secondary consideration, however.)

□ Explore applicable business or professional fraternities for interns.

□ Consider having interns recruit their own replacements. This works well for several reasons:

- The interns know the demands of the job and can find other students who can handle them.
- They feel they are leaving a legacy and will be remembered.
- The incoming interns are motivated to uphold their predecessor's judgment.
- The incoming intern is trained directly by his recruiter.

□ If the replacement recruitment system breaks down for some reason, ask the school placement office for assistance.

Most interns are recruited during the spring semester of their junior year. They work full-time during the following summer and part-time during their senior year. They have an entire summer to learn the job, which makes their part-time work more productive. One-year internships seem best because they give students enough time to become proficient on the job and provide a return on the time invested in their training.

Concerning interviewing the potential replacements, McCarrier says, "The first thing I look for is chemistry. Does the student have the type of personality I can work with? Because we will have to work closely, especially during training, it is essential that we get along."

The next factor is the ability to interact with clerical people of other departments. "This skill is more than just self-confidence," McCarrier says. "Anyone with sufficient self-confidence can learn to work with managers, but the ability to work with the people in the trenches is a rarer commodity. Asking for help from clerical employees is a difficult thing for many college students."

Another important point to consider is how this experience will fit into the student's future career. "Students who plan to go into industrial sales or marketing tend to be excellent because they can see how it will help their careers," says McCarrier. "Those hoping to go into advertising and retailing have not worked out as well, because they have difficulty seeing the practical value of what they are learning on the job."

Assessing Performance

McCarrier's firm has a set policy concerning the intern's pay and performance. "Interns are reviewed quarterly and receive raises every three months. This gives them continuing feedback, and the frequent raises are an excellent morale boost. Because interns are not in the program for more than a year, the added cost is automatically limited," he says.

"We use a two-part evaluation form. The first half is a set of rating scales on specific characteristics, such as dependability and quality of work. The second is a list of four goals that the interns set, such as learning to use a specific PC software package, managing all aspects of a mail survey, or working with the data processing department to develop a new monthly report.

At the end of the quarter, the list is reviewed and a new one is drawn up for the next quarter. This allows interns to work towards goals that are mutually valuable.

"The major problems for the department in having an intern program," McCarrier notes, "are the need to train new people every year and the difficulty in doing rush projects just before final exam week when studying takes priority, or during spring break, when interns want to go home or to Fort Lauderdale. The pace of much of the work in the department is geared to the university's schedule of midterm and final exams, semester breaks, and holidays." Some projects in the market research department can easily be delayed during these periods. "It is simply one aspect of hiring students that must be built into the department's schedule."

"The greatest pay-off for an intern is learning how a business works by watching and being part of it. Concepts presented in class become much more meaningful after seeing them in action. Then, during senior year, job-hunting interns tend to get a lot of second interviews and job offers because they present themselves very well."

Are You Ready for Interns?

The American University's Cooperative Education Program provides an informative question and answer pamphlet, shown in Figure 5-1.

Under the American University program, if employers decide to participate, they are not obligated to hire a student if those interviewed don't fit their needs. The employers provide a description of the available opening, and the University screens candidates. A faculty member approves the position for academic credit, and the office gives the employer a list of possible interviewees.

Another convenient feature is that very little paperwork is involved. All the University requires is a job description and, at the end of the employment period, an evaluation of the student's performance. Through the co-op program, students work full-time or part-time for a 4-month or 6-month period. However, students may work more than one consecutive period or alternate with another student to provide continuous coverage. The pamphlet also notes that intern salaries are determined at the discretion of the employer. However one should keep in mind that many students help to finance their own education and must pay for the academic credits they earn for the co-op experience.

Most universities across the country have a structured internship program, some with more specific requirements and arrangements than others. (See Figures 5-2 through 5-4.) The easiest way to learn what is available is to call your local universities. Ask them to send you information on their internship and career placement programs.

BENEFITS TO PART-TIMERS ABOUND

The benefits the part-timer will receive depend on the desires and motives of the worker. Many are looking for quick dollars, while others want a more flexible schedule than a 9 to 5 job can offer. Still others are investigating new careers, and part-time work is a good way to gain accelerated experience in a short time.

Figure 5-1. The American University Career Center is an example of how colleges can be a good source of reliable employees. Reprinted with permission of The American University.

Participating Curricula:

Accounting	**Engineering**
Administration of Justice	**English**
Police Science	**Geology**
Security Administration	**Government**
Architecture	**History**
Automotive Technology	**Human Services**
Biology	Alcohol Rehabilitation Counseling
Broadcast Journalism	Gerontology
Business Administration	Mental Health
Business Management	Social & Community Services
Chemistry	**Journalism**
Civil Engineering	**Languages**
Commercial Art	**Legal Assisting**
Advertising Design	**Marketing**
Illustration	**Math**
Computer Information Systems	**Music**
Programming	**Office Technologies**
Systems Analysis	**Photography**
Micro Applications	**Physics**
Computer Science	**Psychology**
Construction Management	**Sociology**
Drafting	**Speech/Drama**
Education	**Word Processing**
Early Childhood Development	
Special Education	

Figure 5-1. (continued)

Particular types of employees will receive particular benefits. For the retiree or housewife, part-time work may be a pleasant way to get out of the house for a few hours each day and a chance to feel really productive. High school students may want to enter the working world as early as possible or just do something that interests them a few afternoons a week.

COOPERATIVE EDUCATION
INTERNSHIPS
VOLUNTEER SERVICE/LEARNING
RETIRED VOLUNTEER SERVICE CORPS

EXPERIENTIAL LEARNING PROGRAMS

The University of Maryland welcomes your participation in its Experiential Learning Programs. The ELP office of the College Park campus publishes information about learning opportunities provided by agencies and organizations that offer practical work experiences for students interested in exploring career choices or relating classroom theory to practice. Toward this end, agencies and organizations are invited to participate in three major experiential learning programs.

> VOLUNTEER SERVICE/LEARNING - for experience without pay, the student volunteers in a position related to a major area of study or career interest.

> INTERNSHIP - for academic credit from a faculty member of the University and/or pay from the organization, the student works part-time.

> COOPERATIVE EDUCATION - during alternating semesters/six months, the student works in a full-time position and returns to school alternating semesters/six months.

The enclosed list of majors indicates the broad base of academic experiences which UM students can bring to such organizations as yours.

To participate in Experiential Learning Programs, please complete and return the enclosed forms as soon as possible. Your completed forms will be used to list (by major, position, agency, location, etc.) your opportunities in the ELP computer database, in ELP office catalogs and open files that are easily accessible to students and faculty. The ELP staff will also use the forms to publicize your opportunities by sending announcements to heads of academic departments and, if appropriate, to broadcasters and newspapers on campus.

The ELP staff encourages you to send agency newsletters, brochures, etc. that can be placed in an open file, as well as detailed position descriptions. The staff invites you to call or visit the ELP office any time. If you have questions or any concerns, please don't hesitate to contact us. We're here to help.

Figure 5-2. Information about a state university's student internship program.

ACCOUNTING
ADVERTISING DESIGN
AEROSPACE ENGINEERING
AFRO-AMERICAN STUDIES
AGRI & EXTENSION EDUC
AGRI & RESOURSE ECON
AGRICULTURAL CHEM
AGRICULTURAL ENGR
AGRICULTURAL GENERAL
AGRICULTURE UNDECIDED
AGRONOMY-CROPS
AGRONOMY-SOILS
AGRONOMY-TURF & URBAN AGRO
AMERICAN STUDIES
ANIMAL SCIENCE
ANTHROPOLOGY
APPAREL DESIGN
ARCHITECTURE-B ARCH
ARCHITECTURE-B S
ARCHITECTURE-URBAN STUDIES
ART EDUCATION
ART HISTORY
ART STUDIO
ASTRONOMY
BIOCHEMISTRY
BIOL SCIENCE GENERAL
BIOL SCIENCE-BOTANY
BIOL SCIENCE-ENTOMOLOGY
BIOL SCIENCE-MICROBIOLOGY
BIOL SCIENCE-ZOOLOGY
BIOL SCIENCE-ANIMAL SCIENCES
BOTANY
BUSINESS & MGMT GENERAL
BUSINESS EDUCATION
CHEMICAL ENGINEERING
CHEMISTRY
CIVIL ENGINEERING
COMMUNITY STUDIES
COMPUTER SCIENCE
CONSERVATION AND RESOURCE
  DEVELOPMENT-FISH AND
  WILDLIFE MANAGEMENT
CONS & RES DEV-PLANT
  RESOURCE MANAGEMENT
CONS & RES DEV PEST MGMT
CONS & RES DEV-WATER RES MGMT
CONS & RES DEV-RESOURSE MGMT
CONSUMER ECONOMICS-
  CONSUMER TECHNOLOGY
CRIMINOLOGY
DANCE
DIETETICS
DISTRIBUTIVE EDUCATION
EARLY CHILDHOOD EDUCATION

ECONOMICS
EDUCATION UNDECIDED
ELECTRICAL ENGR
ELEMENTARY EDUCATION
ENGLISH
ENGLISH EDUCATION
ENGINEERING
ENTOMOLOGY
EXPERIMENTAL FOODS
FAMILY STUDIES
FINANCE
FIRE PROTECTION ENGR
FOOD SCIENCE
FOREIGN LANGUAGE EDUC
FRENCH
GENERAL STUDIES PROG
GEOGRAPHY
GEOLOGY
GERMAN & SLAVIC LANG
GOVERNMENT & POLITICS
HEALTH EDUCATION
HEARING & SPEECH SCI
HISTORY
HOME ECONOMICS EDUC
HUMAN ECOLOGY
HORTICULTURE
HOUSING
INDIVIDUAL STUDIES
INDUSTRIAL ARTS EDUC
INDUSTRIAL TECHNOLOGY
INFORMATION SYS MGMT
INSTITUTION ADMINISTN
INTERIOR DESIGN
JEWISH STUDIES
JOURNALISM
KINESIOLOGY SCIENCE
LATIN LANGUAGE & LIT
LAW ENFORCEMENT
LIBRARY SCIENCE EDUC
MANAGEMENT & CONSUMER
  STUDIES
MANAGEMENT SCIENCE &
  STATISTICS
MARKETING
MATHEMATICS
MATHEMATICS EDUCATION
MECHANICAL ENGR
MICROBIOLOGY
MUSIC
MUSIC EDUCATION
MUSIC HISTORY & LIT
MUSIC THEORY & COMP
NUCLEAR ENGINEERING
NUTRITION

PERSONNEL & LABOR RELAT
PHILOSOPHY
PHYSICAL EDUCATION
PHYSICAL SCIENCES
PHYSICS
POULTRY SCIENCE
PRE-ARCHITECTURE
PRE-BUSINESS
PRE-DENTAL HYGIENE
PRE-ENGINEERING
PRE-FORESTRY
PRE-MEDICAL TECHNOLOGY
PRE-NURSING
PRE-PHARMACY
PRE-PHYSICAL THERAPY
PRE-RADIOLOGIC TECHNOLO
PRE-RECREATION
PRE-SPECIAL EDUCATION
PRE-VETERINARY MEDICINE
PRODUCTION MANAGEMENT
PSYCHOLOGY
RADIO TV & FILM
RECREATION
RUSSIAN
RUSSIAN AREA STUDIES
SCIENCE EDUCATION
SECRETARIAL EDUCATION
SOCIAL STUDIES
SOCIOLOGY
SPANISH
SPECIAL EDUCATION
SPEECH & DRAMA EDUCATIO
SPEECH COMMUNICATION
TEXTILE MARKETING
  FASHION MERCHANDISIN
TEXTILES
THEATRE
TRANSPORTATION
URBAN STUDIES
VOCATIONAL TECHNICAL ED
ZOOLOGY

Figure 5-2. (continued)

Employer Responsibilities

1. Designate a Coordinator who has an understanding of, and a strong commitment to the concept of Cooperative Education.
2. Inform the College of available work opportunities.
3. Establish work schedules which accomodate the academic calendar and enable students to meet the requirements of both the College and the employer for completion of the program.
4. Assure that work assignments are closely related to the student's field of study and/or career objectives.
5. Help the student develop a statement of objectives commensurate with the goals of the instructional program and the job activities.
6. Complete and return the quarterly evaluation form provided by the College.
7. Facilitate on-site visits by the College Coordinator.
8. Provide the student employment for at least the minimum number of hours and quarters as arranged by the College and the employer.
9. Establish a salary schedule consistent with minimum wage law and fair employment practices and commensurate with the salary of beginning employees performing comparable functions.
10. Discharge students before the end of the agreed period *only* for just cause or when economic or other factors make continuance impractical or impossible.
11. Terminate a student who fails to register for the Cooperative Education course or who fails to adhere to Cooperative Education policies.
12. Hire permanently *only* students who have graduated or completed the Cooperative Education program as agreed by the College.
13. Inform the College of any change in the student trainee's status.

College Responsibilities

1. Designate a Coordinator to work with the employer's Coordinator for Cooperative Education.
2. Inform students of the employer's Cooperative Education opportunities.
3. Counsel students as to vocational opportunities and help them choose the job most suited to each individual's talents and aspirations.
4. Screen and refer students who meet the College's and the employer's eligibility standards.
5. Correlate work and study in a manner that will assure maximum learning and production on the part of each student.
6. Visit the work site to validate the learning experience and discuss the student's progress with the supervisor and/or employer Coordinator.
7. Evaluate the student for the purpose of assigning academic credit and grade.
8. Provide the employer with the necessary information about the student's field of study, academic standing, progress in the curriculum, proposed date of graduation, and projected work periods.
9. Inform the employer of any change in a student's status including termination of study, change of major, failure to maintain program standards, or withdrawal from program.
10. Return constructive criticism to the employer relative to work assignments, job environment, personality conflicts, and any misunderstandings which may arise.
11. Inform the employer of any student occupying a Cooperative Education position who fails to register for the appropriate Cooperative Education course.
12. Provide any other service that is available at the College and appropriate to the maintenance of a smooth-running and effective Cooperative Education program.

Figure 5-3. A typical breakdown of employer and college responsibitities for a student internship program.

EMPLOYER'S EVALUATION OF COOPERATIVE STUDENT

Name _____ Major _____ Work Period _____

Employer _____ Location _____

INSTRUCTIONS: The immediate supervisor should evaluate the student objectively, comparing him with other students of comparable academic level, with other personnel assigned the same or similarly classified jobs, or with individual standards. *Remarks are particularly helpful.*

ATTITUDE—APPLICATION TO WORK
- ☐ Outstanding in enthusiasm
- ☐ Very interested and industrious
- ☐ Average in diligence and interest
- ☐ Somewhat indifferent
- ☐ Definitely not interested

ABILITY TO LEARN
- ☐ Learned work exceptionally well
- ☐ Learned work readily
- ☐ Average in understanding work
- ☐ Rather slow in learning
- ☐ Very slow to learn

DEPENDABILITY
- ☐ Completely dependable
- ☐ Above average in dependability
- ☐ Usually dependable
- ☐ Sometimes neglectful or careless
- ☐ Unreliable

INITIATIVE
- ☐ Proceeds well on his own
- ☐ Goes ahead independently at times
- ☐ Does all assigned work
- ☐ Hesitates
- ☐ Must be pushed frequently

QUALITY OF WORK
- ☐ Excellent
- ☐ Very good
- ☐ Average
- ☐ Below average
- ☐ Very poor

RELATIONS WITH OTHERS
- ☐ Exceptionally well accepted
- ☐ Works well with others
- ☐ Gets along satisfactorily
- ☐ Has difficulty working with others
- ☐ Works very poorly with others

MATURITY—POISE
- ☐ Quite poised and confident
- ☐ Has good self-assurance
- ☐ Average maturity and poise
- ☐ Seldom asserts himself
- ☐ Timid   ☐ Brash

QUANTITY OF WORK
- ☐ Unusually high output
- ☐ More than average
- ☐ Normal amount
- ☐ Below average
- ☐ Low out-put, slow

JUDGMENT
- ☐ Exceptionally mature in judgment
- ☐ Above average in making decisions
- ☐ Usually makes the right decision
- ☐ Often uses poor judgment
- ☐ Consistently uses bad judgment

ATTENDANCE: ☐ Regular ☐ Irregular | **PUNCTUALITY:** ☐ Regular ☐ Irregular

OVER-ALL PERFORMANCE:

Outstanding	Very Good	+	Average	–	Marginal	Unsatisfactory

The student's technical abilities, personal qualities, and other job related attributes are:

The areas which the student should strive to most improve are:

For additional remarks, please use reverse side.

Has report been discussed with the student?   ☐ Yes   ☐ No
(We encourage employers to discuss this evaluation with the student.)

(Signed) _____ (Date) _____
                (Immediate Supervisor)

Figure 5-4. Form to be used by an employer in evaluating the progress of a student intern.

EMPLOYER'S PROGRESS REPORT
OF
COOPERATIVE EDUCATION PARTICIPANT

Student's Name _____   Date_____

Employer _____   Student's Position:

_____

Student's Supervisor _____

Student's Curriculum:

Please Rate the Student According to the Following:

_____

	Superior	Good	Average	Below Average	Unsatis-factory
Attitude Toward Work					
Quantity of Work Accomplished					
Quality of Work					
Professional Growth on the Job					
Ability to Get Along with Others					
Growth in Self Confidence					
Willingness to Learn					
Ability to Communicate					
Tact, Poise, Courtesy					
Dependability					
Conformance to Rules and Regulations					
Potential for Leadership					

Letter Grade you feel the student has earned during this quarter _____

Please comment on the student's strengths and/or weaknesses. Include other comments you would like to make.

_____

_____

_____

Signature of Evaluator _____   Date_____

Figure 5-4. (continued)

Regular part-time employees may be looking for full-time jobs. College students who may have held various jobs during high school may be testing possible careers. They can gain a business vocabulary before leaving college. Other motivations include paying their way through college or accumulating a super resume with key endorsements before graduation. The big plus for everyone is that the student may become a full-time employee after graduation—a real bonus if he is already experienced in helping with your marketing program.

6

YELLOW PAGE ADVERTISING THAT GETS NOTICED

If you stop being better, you stop being good.

Oliver Cromwell

This chapter and the one that follows discuss how to get maximum return for the dollars invested in what are generally mandatory marketing vehicles for most businesses. While neither Yellow Pages advertisements nor brochures are inherently inexpensive from the shoestring marketer's standpoint, both can be used to get more mileage out of expenditures.

History of the Yellow Pages

The first telephone directory, a single page listing names of customers of the New Haven District Telephone Company, was published in 1878. Five years later, a printer in Cheyenne ran out of white paper and substituted the yellow paper from which this advertising medium would take its name. By 1906, Yellow Pages published by the Michigan State Telephone Company in Detroit were similar enough to today's style to be called their forerunner.

Today, advertising in the Yellow Pages is big business. Between 1980 and 1985, the Yellow Pages' growth in consumer advertising revenue surpassed that of all other media except direct mail. A

Whirlpool Corporation study showed that, next to the recommendations of family and friends, people most often turn to the Yellow Pages for information on products and services they've already decided they need. More than 90% of adults use Yellow Pages directories for a total of four billion references each year.

DECISIONS ABOUT USING YELLOW PAGES

Yellow Pages are directional media, showing people where to buy once they have already made the decision. Before 1984, advertisers had only a few decisions to make: whether or not to advertise in the Yellow Pages and, if so, which headings to use, how large an ad to run, and what type of layout would be most effective.

With the increased number of directories available in many markets, a result of the AT&T divestiture ruling, advertisers also must choose which directory to use. A few large cities now have as many as 12 Yellow Pages serving them.

To help you make the decision, first ask the publishers of each local Yellow Pages directory for a complete media kit. This should include information on circulation figures and costs for different sizes of ads. A standard industry source of media usage data, Simmons Market Research Bureau (SMRB), at 219 East 42nd Street, New York, NY 10017, provides data on consumer and business-to-business use of the Yellow Pages.

Another information source is Statistical Research, Incorporated (SRI), 111 Prospect Street, Westfield, NJ 07090. They conduct studies of consumer and business users of the Yellow Pages. Commissioned by the American Association of Yellow Pages Publishers, they provide detailed information on characteristics of consumer and business users, rate of use, reasons for using, and other relevant information. To learn more about these and other studies contact the American Association of Yellow Page Publishers, 500 Chesterfield Center, Suite 250, Chesterfield, MO 63017, (314)532-6515.

Independent research conducted in 1985 found that 98% of consumers use the Yellow Pages an average of 36 times per year. SMRB discovered that:

□ 83.6% of all adults consult the Yellow Pages when they're considering a purchase.

□ Nationwide, more than 62 million adults consult the Yellow Pages in an average week.

□ Among total references to the Yellow Pages, 38.7% occur when an individual does not have a specific name in mind but is simply beginning to search for a product or service.

□ Among total references to the Yellow Pages, 82.9% result in contacts.

□ 61.5% of adults use the Yellow Pages at their place of business.

□ In a one-month period, 69.7% of adults aged 25-34 used the Yellow Pages at home or elsewhere.

□ 74.7% of those using the Yellow Pages have college degrees.

□ 73.4% of all professionals or managers used the Yellow Pages.

□ 70% had an income of $30,000 or more and 67.8% lived in homes valued at more than $60,000.

People who refer to the Yellow Pages are in the mood to buy a product or use a service. They generally have made a purchasing decision and now are trying to determine where to look for the item or service. Thus, they are a select audience.

Who Publishes the Yellow Pages?

Utility related publishers compile Yellow Pages directories for the telephone companies, and independent publishers, some of whom have been in business for many years, produce directories tailored to specific market segments. Depending on the size of your community, there may be as many as six different directories targeted at various markets. For instance, individual directories may be aimed at the elderly, college students, women, and industrial buyers.

Since the ruling requiring divestiture by AT&T, competition has increased markedly between publishers owned by Bell Telephone and independent publishers. Traditionally, advertising in directories produced in affiliation with Bell Telephone was the best buy regardless of cost. However, independent publishers often can offer lower rates and premiums. Many publishers also invite you to advertise through the "Green Pages"—a section in the middle of the phone directory in which companies offer discount coupons. (See Figure 6-1.)

You should request advertising rate cards from each of the Yellow Pages publishers in your area and compare the circulation, the advertising fee, and the anticipated life of each Yellow Pages directory. Representatives from the Yellow Pages directories in your area may work directly with you, helping design your ads and supplying you with data on the people who use their directories. Local sales of Yellow Pages advertising space account for 90% of their sales.

Support From National Advertisers

Campaigns by Yellow Pages publishers recently have touted the benefits of cooperative advertising. (More on this in Chapter 12.) Out of $7 billion available each year for "co-op" advertising, approximately $1.8 billion is approved for use with Yellow Pages ads. In such advertising, the cost is shared between the national advertiser and the local retailer. Check with your suppliers to determine if co-op funds are available for the products you sell.

Next, determine whether your business qualifies for co-op funds. Many programs have minimum purchase requirements and specific time periods within which you need to make these purchases. You also will also need to review the requirements of the co-op program you plan to use. There will be guidelines for developing the ad and using the manufacturer's logo, and other information you'll need to create an acceptable ad. Depending on the specific co-op program, you will find that the manufacturer may reimburse you for up to 100% of your space cost in the Yellow Pages.

If your suppliers are not aware of cooperative advertising, point out the advantages of having their names in hundreds of local Yellow Pages. Since the cost generally is split between you and your supplier, a Yellow Pages ad can give you both improved visibility at a reasonable cost.

10% OFF 3 TO 5 HOURS
15% OFF 6 – 8 HOURS
- MUST BE PRESENTED AT TIME OF RESERVATION
- NOT VALID FOR PROMS -
GEORGETOWN LIMOUSINE SERVICE
533-8663 EXP 5/88
SERVING ENTIRE METRO AREA

COUPON

10% OFF
PERSONALIZED BANNER
FOR YOUR SPECIAL EVENT
659-6290
1 COUPON PER CUSTOMER
EXPIRES 7-31-88
REDEEMABLE AT TIME OF PAYMENT

COUPON

AUTO SOUND ELECTRONICS

25% OFF ON OUR CAR STEREO INSTALLATION
WITH PURCHASE OF CAR STEREO
1 COUPON PER PURCHASE
NOT GOOD ON ANY OTHER OFFERS
EXPIRES 1-1-88
3220 OLD LEE HWY FAIRFAX
SEE OUR AD UNDER AUTO RADIOS FOR DIRECTIONS
385-2886

COUPON

DISCOUNT REFRIGERATION & APPLIANCE CO.
CALL 8AM TO 8PM MON – SAT
GOOD FOR REFRIGERATORS – STOVES – WASHERS
DRYERS – DISHWASHERS – MICROWAVES
10% OFF ALL SERVICE WORK
- ONE COUPON PER CUSTOMER - EXPIRES 4/30/88
- NOT GOOD WITH OTHER OFFERS
SERVING ENTIRE METRO AREA **386-3350** SERVING ENTIRE NO. VA.

COUPON

ZAP TYPE
10% OFF
YOUR FIRST ORDER OF $50.00 OR MORE
SEE OUR DISPLAY AD UNDER PRINTERS
2029 K STREET N.W.
LOWER LEVEL **775-4898**
ONE COUPON PER CUSTOMER OFFER EXPIRES MAY 1988

COUPON

ZAP TYPE
10% OFF
YOUR FIRST ORDER OF $50.00 OR MORE
SEE OUR DISPLAY AD UNDER WORD PROCESSING SERVICES
2029 K STREET N.W.
LOWER LEVEL **775-4898**
ONE COUPON PER CUSTOMER OFFER EXPIRES MAY 1988

COUPON

TYSONS CORNER TRANSMISSION CENTER
"Over 27 Years At The Same Location" "Factory Trained Mechanics"
$25 OFF
COMPLETE
TRANSMISSION OVERHAUL
TOWING AVAILABLE
"ASK ABOUT OUR CONDITIONAL GUARANTEE"
893-7335
- ONLY 1 COUPON PER CUSTOMER
- MUST BE PRESENTED AT TIME OF SALE
- NOT GOOD WITH ANY OTHER ADVERTISED OFFER
- EXPIRES 5-31-88
8346 LEESBURG PIKE (RT 7) TYSONS CORNER
(DIRECTLY ACROSS FROM JKJ CHEV. - BEHIND MERCHANTS TIRE)

COUPON

WINDOWS
10% OFF ANY JOB
— Aluminum & Vinyl Windows —
Sales – Installation – Service
CARLSON BUILDERS INC
731-0284
Expires 5-30-88 - One Coupon Per Customer
Not Good With Any Other Offer - Present At Time Of Sale

COUPON

POLYNESIA N' THINGS
$5 OFF ONE VISIT
"DISCOVER THE DIFFERENCE"
740 7TH ST SE WASHINGTON
MAJOR CREDIT CARDS
OPEN 7 DAYS A WEEK
SEE OUR DISPLAY AD – MASSAGE
LIMIT ONE COUPON PER CUSTOMER
EXPIRES 6/30/88
546-1492

COUPON

H&R TOWING SERVICE
RADIO DISPATCHED - QUICK RESPONSE
Bethesda Downtown
656-5607 966-9566

20% OFF
- LOCAL TOWING
- JUMP STARTS
- TIRE CHANGES
Exp. 7-31-88
- Coupon Not Valid
With Any Other Offer
Or Discounts.

Figure 6-1. Money-saving coupons are a new and popular feature in many Yellow Pages directories. Reprinted with permission.

Advertising rates, which vary widely from one market to another, are dependent on conditions in your marketplace. For example, running a quarter-column display ad in 1987 in the Brooklyn, New York Yellow Pages would cost $2545.90 whereas the same ad in Frostproof, Florida would cost $172.80.

The Mini Yellow Pages

Since the break-up of AT&T, there has been a proliferation of mini Yellow Pages: small directories, 1/4" thick, focusing on a specific locale. (See sample cover, Figure 6-2.) Mini Yellow Pages harbor both advantages and disadvantages. Among the advantages are:

1. **Lower prices.** Many of the small independents offer advertising rates averaging 30% to 40% below the larger Bell-operated companies.

2. **More flexibility.** Because the scope of the operations behind the mini Yellow Pages is smaller, you will not have to fuss with the bureaucracy associated with the larger companies. Unlike the Bell-operated companies, the local Yellow Pages entrepreneur generally does not have to answer to anyone but her better judgment. This added flexibility allows you to be more creative.

3. **More colorful artwork.** Although most mini Yellow Pages offer only yellow and black, many have added extra colors to out-do the larger publications. Red and green tend to be the primary third colors available. If a mini Yellow Pages in your area offers this eye-catching service, it is to your advantage to use it.

4. **Coupons.** Some Yellow Pages include a coupon section in the book. This section allows the advertiser to further his marketing efforts by giving the consumer added motivation to use his product or service, such as discounts or free services. Coupons also refer readers to the display ad in the main directory.

5. **Ad development help.** While the big Yellow Pages will provide sales representatives to help you develop your ad, the

Figure 6-2. A typical mini-directory serving residents and businesses in a particular neighborhood or locality. Reprinted with permission.

smaller ones are able to give you more personalized attention without the pressure that the big guys use to push you into a larger ad. After you have gained experience with the mini Yellow Pages you will be better able to deal with the faster pace of the traditional Yellow Pages.

6. **Local orientation.** Community directories deal more effectively with the needs of the residents. If you are searching for a barber shop close to home, looking through a large metropolitan Yellow Pages can be frustrating and time consuming. Instead, your community directory will contain entries only for barber shops in your section of town.

7. **Better grade of paper.** Because these books are smaller, their paper is heavier. This makes the book more attractive to a customer who does not want to deal with ripped, fly-away pages. It also decreases the amount of type that shows through from the other side of the page.

8. **Local FYI.** This category includes any information about the community that will add to the convenience and utility of the book. Such items as maps, public transportation guides, special events calendars, schedules for local sports teams, seating charts of arenas and major theaters, household hints, historical dates, and community points of interest are all pluses over the larger competitors.

Unfortunately, the mini Yellow Pages are not without drawbacks. The main ones include:

1. **Not well established.** By the very nature of a growing market, many of the participants are new companies. Because of this, few have much of a track record and some risk is involved when handing over your money to one of these young enterprises. To minimize this risk, contact your local consumer agency or ask for references before you invest.

2. **Distribution channels.** Because the small independents do not have access to the vast distribution channels like those of the Bell-operated companies, their distribution is often less complete. Also, as opposed to the large directories, the small companies obtain little or no feedback from residents who did

not receive a copy of the directory. After all, how can you miss something that you do not know exists?

3. **Retainability.** It is difficult to measure just how many people keep the mini directories they receive each year. Because storage space tends to be tight, some may choose simply to rely on their old, familiar Yellow Pages. Also, because the mini directories are so small, they are much easier to throw away or misplace.

Another spin-off from the traditional Yellow Pages are the specialty pages. These books are tailored to a specific market or audience. The most popular are Yellow Pages aimed at women (see Figure 6-3), Hispanics, and blacks.

The specialty directory that has enjoyed the greatest amount of success nationwide is Southwestern Bell's *Silver Pages*. In several U.S. markets, this directory targets the growing over-60 population through special offers and discounts. The problem of gaining credibility was surmounted when Southwestern won the support of several agencies that serve the elderly. In addition, the directories inform their readers of programs and services available for the aging.

USING THE YELLOW PAGES TO YOUR GREATEST ADVANTAGE

Unlike an advertisement in a weekly or monthly publication, the decisions you make when designing your Yellow Pages ad will represent your company for a full year. You first must decide which directory to use.

Your Yellow Pages publisher or sales representative should be able to give you usage data for the directory. Remember to ask about the type of distribution system the publisher uses. Do they mail copies or deliver door-to-door? Do they give businesses one copy for each telephone on the premises? In addition to the factors discussed above, geographic area covered plays an important role. Do most of your customers come from within a five-mile radius of your place of business? Or do you draw customers from a wide radius inside your metropolitan area?

1987
Edition

THE WASHINGTON METROPOLITAN
WOMEN'S YELLOW PAGES

AN ANNUAL DIRECTORY
OF WASHINGTON METROPOLITAN AREA
WOMEN'S BUSINESSES AND SERVICES

P.O. BOX 1737
ALEXANDRIA, VA 22314
(703) 548-1333

Figure 6-3. An example of the new breed of specialty Yellow Pages—this one
designed to meet the needs of women. Reprinted with the permission
of Women's Yellow Pages.

Does your product or service apply to a small, specialized target market or to a larger population? Also, where are your competitors advertising? Have they been long-term users of that directory? If so, it's a good bet they are getting results.

Your Yellow Pages entry is in competition with others who advertise in your general product or service area. You will need to create an approach for your advertisement that makes it stand out from all the others and that creates a highly favorable image. If you rely on your name, address and phone number alone, you risk being overlooked. If you use bland wording and tired graphics, others will outshine you easily.

The ad's effectiveness should be your final decision point. After all, the ad must work.

Your Ad's Purpose

An often forgotten element in planning a Yellow Pages advertisement is determining its purpose. What do you want to accomplish? Do you want to appear more substantial than you are? Do you want to create an image (i.e., of high quality, caring service, convenience, low prices)? Do you want to distinguish yourself from the competition? Do you want to announce the availability of certain products or services not available elsewhere in your general area?

With your own purpose in mind, you can begin to look for other advertisements that seem to serve similar purposes. Ask yourself: What is it about this advertisement that makes the establishment appear substantial? What is it about this one that gives it a high class image? Why did my eye fall on this ad before all the others in its category? Then start writing.

The Directory Heading.   Your next choice will be the heading under which your company name should appear. For a plywood dealer, *Plywood & Veneers—Retail* may be obvious and appropriate. For a small contractor, *Home Improvements* may be appropriate. An appliance dealer will quickly select *Appliances* or *Electronic Equipment and Supplies*.

Think of other possibilities, suggests Alan D. Fletcher, professor of advertising at Louisiana State University. An informal study of your customers establishes some surprising categories. Your customers may be fixing a house and not be aware of the different types of materials available. Listing yourself under *Building Materials* will bring you the customers who didn't know they wanted to use plywood in the first place.

Public relations counselors probably can be listed under *Advertising Agencies and Counselors*, as well as under *Public Relations*. The company listed under *Home Improvements* can also be listed under *Electricians, Plumbers and Roofing Contractors*. The appliance dealer should be listed under several of these headings: *Television Dealers, Television Service, Microwave Ovens, Tape Recorders, Refrigerators and Freezers, Dishwashing Machines.*

Providing General Information. You'll need to provide enough information to give your business some appeal and interest, but not so much that nobody wants to read it all. Readers of Yellow Pages advertisements want to know your name, location, phone number, and just a few of the most outstanding features about your business. The "outstanding features" information is that which you think will draw customers, such as free estimates, free parking, location next to Zoro Supermarket, all bonded workers, 24-hour emergency service, same day services, pick-up and delivery, and other such drawing cards.

Consider including your hours of business and, if you are in a location that is not well known, a small map (see Figure 6-4).

A good informational device is a single phrase that describes your business, usually placed near the top of the ad, right under the business name. If possible, work into that phrase such catch words as *quality, complete, reliable, fast* and *dependable* if they are important in your line of business. For example, your phrase might be: "Complete furniture repair and remodeling services" or "High quality printing at discount prices."

Size and Format. The Yellow Pages industry offers a wide variety of advertising sizes and formats. The table on page 88 shows the format designations that most publishers recognize. To decide which format and size will be best for you, first research the advertisements placed by your competitors. What is the smallest size that catches your eye and doesn't get lost among the others?

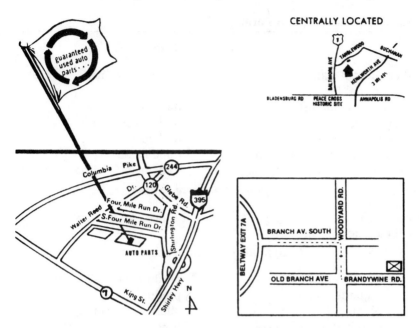

Figure 6-4. A simple map in your Yellow Pages ad can guide customers directly to your door.

When you do this, think in terms of columns and inches. Yellow Pages generally use a four-column format (four columns of print run across the page). Most ads run across one or two columns and may be anywhere from just an inch to several inches deep. Obviously, larger ads have a greater chance of being noticed, but you'll need to weigh size against how much money you want to spend and how much information you need to present in the ad.

However, don't let your ad be so small that it has no more impact than a simple bold entry for your name, address, and phone number. Will buying a quarter column place you on the same level as your competitors or will you overshadow them? Do most of your competitors use cross references listed in bold face type?

Type Styles and Sizes. When you scan the Yellow Pages, which styles of type catch your eye? Bold italic? All capital letters? Type that leans left or right? How big is the type, especially in ads that are the same size as your ad will be? In general, it is best to

Yellow Pages Sizes and Formats

Trade Items and Listings

alternate call listing	custom trademark
anchor bold listing	extra line
anchor semibold listing	trade bold listing
bold listing	trade cross reference
cross reference bold listing	trademark
cross reference regular listing	trade name
cross reference semibold listing	trade name alternate call listing

Options for Space Listing

1 space listing	2 inch space listing, etc.
1 inch space listing	

Options for Column Displays

double half column	product sell, half column
double quarter column	product sell, quarter column
half column	quarter column
product sell, double half column	triple quarter column
product sell, double quarter column	product sell, triple quarter column, etc.

strive for a clean, easily read style, with your company name in a type that is bolder and at least twice as large as the rest of the type in your ad.

When you are writing the advertisement, you will be concerned with the ad heading, the copy for your ad, the inclusion of your company's name, address, and telephone number, and the use of artwork that will reinforce your sales message.

The Ad Heading.   The heading should draw attention to your business. If the name of your company is descriptive, and indicates your business, like "Johnson Engineering," then its use would be appropriate.

Use the prominence of your heading to help attract attention to your ad and to the sales message it presents. "Clogged Drain?," "Printing While You Wait," "We Service All Makes," and similar headings help catch a potential customer's attention when he's searching through the Yellow Pages.

Your Ad Copy. In your ad copy, you want to tell potential customers what products or services you offer and distinguish yourself from your competitors. If your company offers a wide range of goods or services, you may want to include phrases like "All Major Brands." On the other hand, if you specialize, use words like "Specialists in Foreign Cars." Then list other aspects of your business that set you apart from the others.

Do you offer delivery, in-store financing, expert installation, lifetime guarantees, or any other special attraction? You can also provide sales-oriented information about your company itself, since many people may not be familiar with your name. "Serving Greater Pittsburgh since 1955," "Over 200,000 Satisfied Customers," or "Member of the Cincinnati Chamber of Commerce" helps instill confidence.

Your Company's Name. Your ad should clearly tell people the name of your business. You also may want to use your company logo and list your hours.

Borders. You'll notice all sorts of borders around advertisements, and some do a good job of setting an ad apart from neighboring ads and phone listings. In general, those using heavy black lines or double lines draw more attention than those using thin lines. Rounded corners also can attract attention, since they are not used with great frequency.

Some establishments use borders as identification. Lumber companies use borders drawn to resemble wood planking and fence companies use borders that look like chain link. These and other devices can easily look cluttered. If you decide to use border art, be careful to use adequate white space within the ad.

Logos. If you have a logo, definitely use it in all of your advertising. This is a good way to build identification. Most logos fit best in a corner, but some may look fine centered at the top or bottom of your ad. You'll need to size your logo so that it is recognizable without overwhelming the rest of your entry.

You'll notice many ads, especially for retail establishments, that include the logos of brands they carry or of credit cards they honor. Use these only if you think they are really a draw for your establishment and will distinguish it from others. For example, if yours is the only plumbing contracting company in your area that honors credit cards, you may want to draw attention to this; but if your business is a restaurant, acceptance of credit cards is not an unusual feature worthy of attention.

White Space.   The amount of space within your borders not occupied by type or artwork is an important visual consideration. Most advertisers are tempted to fill up the space they pay for, but this is a mistake. Plenty of white space is necessary to let your ad, and the information in it, stand out from the surrounding columns of type. White space contrasts well with heavy borders and bold headline type, and it helps to prevent a cluttered look.

Look for ads that are the same size as the one you plan to place and see how much white space is used in those that catch your eye.

Layout.   Since normal eye movement is from left to right, present your ad elements in a flush left pattern instead of a flush right. However, a flush right layout can work well when copy is in point rather than sentence form. Illustrative materials should lead the eye into your ad copy. Poorly placed copy breaks the eye's normal path and is hard to follow.

The most obvious way to balance an ad is to center everything, but such symmetry is neither lively nor easy to read.

The Telephone Number.   Many businesses, particularly in the last five years, have used vanity telephone numbers to help customers find and remember them. In 1982, I paid a little extra and had my phone number converted to (703) 931-1984. If you're a baker, why not use 73-BAKER or, if your exchange permits, COOKIES. Photographers can use 42-PHOTO, and so on.

Here are some additional do's and don'ts from the American Association of Yellow Pages Publishers to use when designing your Yellow Pages advertisement:

Do:

□ Think from the reader's point of view. For your business, does the customer need more than just the telephone number? Hours of operation? Lines carried? Location?

□ Distinguish your business from the competition. Are your years in business important to customers?

□ Make it easy for the reader to find you. A local landmark may help: "One block west of Palace Movie Theatre."

□ Keep the ad clean and simple.

Don't:

□ Use the company name as the heading unless it is descriptive.

□ Use more than two different type faces.

□ Use detailed line drawings.

□ Use color photographs or poorly focused black-and-white pictures.

Checking Your Return on Investment

At some point you'll need to evaluate the effectiveness of your advertising dollars in the Yellow Pages. The simplest method for doing so is to total the number of telephone inquiries you receive from Yellow Pages. Ask your customers such questions as "How did you first hear about us?" and "Did you see our ad in the Yellow Pages?"

According to various studies, only 30% of Yellow Pages advertisers keep track of the amount of business their ads are bringing them. Stress the importance of doing so to your employees.

A second, more expensive method is to use a special telephone line with a number that appears only in the Yellow Pages advertisement. When that line rings, it is clear that the Yellow Pages generated the call. To reduce the cost of using this method, you can arrange to have the last line on your business telephone adjusted so that calls on other lines do not "roll over" to it. You then can list the number of the last line in your Yellow Pages ads in order to obtain the same information.

A third method is to use a line of advertising copy that offers a discount. Many Yellow Pages publishers will allow a line such as "Ask Pamela for our special discount" or "Mention this ad and receive a special discount."

Toll-Free 800 Numbers

In addition to numerous other customer lures, toll-free numbers can be a useful tool in your Yellow Pages advertising. Toll-free 800 numbers have become an excellent marketing tool and have greatly improved customer relations. By allowing the customer to call you without bearing the costs himself, toll-free numbers open a direct, worry-free channel of communication.

Although you may not find a need to include this feature in a local Yellow Pages ad, it will come in handy when advertising in a metropolitan Yellow Pages. Many of these super-sized directories cover several outlying areas that require a long distance call to reach. Including your toll-free number in such a directory would encourage potential customers who are a little further away to give you a call.

Many enterprising small businesses have used toll-free numbers to their advantage. Not only has this service improved customer relations, it has also expanded small business markets. For example, one of my researchers, Erin Austin, interned with a sports marketing firm that placed tennis professionals with racquet clubs. Although the business originally was centralized in one metropolitan area, the president, himself a former tennis professional, soon had visions of expanding his operation nationwide. Realizing many people are reluctant to waste money on a long-distance call when they are simply gathering information, the president quickly acquired toll-free service to encourage both clubs and tennis pros from everywhere in the U.S. to contact him. His company now supplies sports personnel to more than 120 clubs across the country.

Procter and Gamble, which relies heavily on its refined 800 system, lists four major advantages of toll-free access:

1. It enables you to respond to each caller's specific need as it arises.

2. The customer receives personalized and more satisfying attention by communicating with you directly.
3. Because the phone response is immediate, the frustration and disillusionment of waiting for a written response is avoided.
4. The cost of the phone call is less than the cost in labor hours needed to write a letter in response.

In addition, surveys reveal that ads with a toll-free number receive a 20% higher "seen" score than comparable ads without it. Most importantly, both the customer and the company benefit from the use of a toll-free 800 number.

Although AT&T once enjoyed a monopoly in the toll-free service market, it recently has been challenged by one likely competitor, with another on the horizon. In early 1987, MCI Communications Corporation announced the availability of its own toll-free service. The best part of the news is that its services will be priced competitively at an average of 10% less than AT&T's service. MCI also plans to undercut AT&T by not tacking on additional charges for several complementary services.

MCI recognized the market potential for this service, which is increasing at a significantly faster rate than overall long-distance service. US Sprint Communications also has responded to the increased demand and expects to offer a similar toll-free service by the end of 1987. Probabilities are high that this third competitor will drive costs down even further to make this service an attractive marketing option for your business.

A Picture (But Not a Photo) Is Worth a Thousand Words

As mentioned earlier, pictures are excellent attention getters, but not every picture is necessarily a winner. While a picture is worth a thousand words, there is no guarantee that those words will be flattering. A picture that creates a positive image can work wonders, but a picture that fails can do a great deal of harm. For this reason, you must be very careful when choosing a picture or illustration for your advertisement. Avoid photographs in your Yellow Pages ad—they just don't work.

To illustrate this point, let's compare two ads from a metropolitan Yellow Pages featuring beauty salons (see Figure 6-5).

These ads, as well as several others presented throughout this book, will be reprinted with names, addresses, and phone numbers obscured to protect the guilty.

The first ad has several elements in its favor. The ad demands attention. The salon uses the signature of the hairdresser as a recognizable symbol. The slant of the type sets the ad apart from the others on the page. The content of the ad is also very appealing. The advertiser has successfully detailed the services offered with colorful descriptions and encouraging phrases. The ad conveys the prestige attached to the salon and plays upon this in its logo.

The picture provides further impact. The profile of a beautifully groomed woman adds to the air of elegance. Her perfectly styled hair conveys a chic and elegant image. The picture associates the salon with the quality of work and the standards of the clientele. It tells the consumer that this is not the place for a mohawk haircut or an inexpensive shampoo. It targets a mature, upperclass audience, while immediately assuring them of professional, quality service.

In contrast, let's look at the second ad. It not only lacks "umph," but it could scare customers away. Granted, the salon may be appealing to a different target group. Still, the structure of the ad is boring and unimaginative. The heaviness of the type subtracts from the name of the salon. Nothing in particular grabs your attention. The services are listed so bluntly they give the impression that the salon experience is an unpleasant one. The photo used in this advertisement is particularly damaging. This photo contrasts with the picture used in the first advertisement.

The thousand words that the two pictures speak are worlds apart. The first ad implies that a visit to the salon is a luxury, while the second leaves the sting of hairspray in your eye.

Figure 6-6 shows another set of advertisements found in a small community Yellow Pages directory. The two boutiques chose very different techniques for advertising their merchandise.

The XYZ Boutique chose a simple, to-the-point advertisement. The name of the boutique is set in small type—even smaller and less noticeable than the address. The description of the merchandise is flat and unresponsive. Unfortunately for the advertiser, the ad leaves the impression that the clothes and accessories offered are as drab and boring as the advertisement.

Figure 6-5. Two Yellow Page ads for similar service companies—one that's attractive, and one that's less so.

95

Figure 6-6 Compare these two Yellow Pages listings. Which is more appealing?

The ad for DEF Boutique uses the same amount of space to its advantage. The name is set in bold, eye-catching type. The drawing of a fashionable young woman is very effective in expressing a stylish clothing collection. The advertiser employs excellent word choice for the ad copy. Highly descriptive adjectives have been selected to enhance the image of DEF Boutique. The combination used works in two ways: while tooting its own horn, it decreases the visibility of XYZ gala's advertisement, which blends into the page with the rest of the one-line advertisements.

THE YELLOW PAGES SCAN

To be competitive, use what the competition has done to improve your own ad. The Yellow Pages scan is one of the best and most efficient ways to start developing your own Yellow Pages advertisement. It involves a minute bit of research on your part, but the rewards are well worth your efforts. In a nutshell, collect impressive advertisements from around the country in your industry and extract "the best of the best" to help form your own winner.

Get your hands on the Yellow Pages of various large cities. I would suggest New York, Los Angeles, Chicago, and Dallas. You probably do not have a copy of these books in your home or office; however, you can easily gain access to them through a local public or college library. Some libraries stock the actual Yellow Pages while others have copies on microfiche, called *Phonefiche*. In either case, a librarian will provide assistance if needed.

The next step is to perform the scan. Look under the appropriate heading, flip through the ads, and note those that really impress you. If you are reading actual Yellow Pages copies, use a paper clip to mark the page so it can be easily found for photocopying later. If you are viewing microfiche, be sure to use a viewer that doubles as a copier–you can make the copies as you come upon a likely inclusion.

Once you have made copies of all the ads you would like to use in the scan, if there is one available, a bulletin board is a very effective means of displaying the ads for review that you have collected. If one is not available, use your desk or even the dining room table for the next step.

Spread out the ads that you will be using to facilitate the review process. Now, using your personal taste and the guidelines provided at the beginning of the chapter, pick out the features that appeal to you most. Make a list of these features for future reference. This list should include: bordering, type, highlights, page placement, illustrations, information, and size and shape of the ad. You probably have some unique ideas of your own that you did not find in your sample ads. Use them. No one knows your business better than you do.

Next, put your artistic abilities to work. Although this step does not require a degree in commercial art, it does require a few elementary tools and lots of imagination. You will need paper, a pencil, a ruler, tape, and scissors. With these items you can experiment with your potential Yellow Pages ad. Decide on a general size and shape. Notice how I used "general." Remember, you are experimenting, so feel free to change either of these elements as you go along.

Look at the ads you have selected and choose a size and shape you find suitable—and affordable—for your advertising objective. Tru-Test Paints has used a paint can to embody its advertising message (Figure 6-7). This irregular shape causes the ad to stand apart from the other paint ads.

After choosing a size and shape, designate one piece of paper to be the background of the ad and place all the details on this. When you have created something you think you would like to use, cut it out and place it within the borders of the ad. Now you can easily rearrange the ad as many times as you like.

Consider the most important element of your ad—your business' name. How would you like it to appear? Do you prefer elegance or a wholesome appearance? Depending on your line of

Figure 6-7. Clever use of an eye-catching and appropiate shape for a Yellow Pages ad. Reprinted with permission.

business, either style may be appropriate. Check what the competition is using and what you deem to be the most impressive. You may want to clip out the name of the company whose heading pleases you most. Place this as a substitute in the ad where you would like your name to be.

Continue this process with any bits of information you would like to include in your advertisement. Refer to your list of desirable elements that you would like to include in your ad. But be careful not to clutter the ad and decrease it effectiveness.

Keep working on your ad for a while, then look at it again a few days later. A layout that looks good both today and tomorrow probably is good!

7

ADVERTISING IN BUSINESS DIRECTORIES

I have failed to take advantage of many opportunities, but the world has not failed in offering them.

Edgar W. Howe

If you are in the business of providing products or services to other businesses, particularly on a nationwide basis, then this chapter could be of great interest to you. We will explore the world of business directories and how they enhance your other marketing efforts.

Philip O'Keefe, president of a consulting firm in Glenridge, New Jersey, believes that many companies can effectively "get discovered with directories." According to O'Keefe, "If you are going to have a balanced marketing plan, you have got to consider the often slighted realm of advertising in business directories. Sharp planning can strengthen your directory ad program."

"The keys to an effective program for advertising in business directories are setting objectives, using creative techniques, and measuring results," says O'Keefe. This chapter is based on O'Keefe's observations and expertise as a consultant on projects involving advertising in directories and in various Yellow Pages.

Directory advertising is growing rapidly, perhaps faster than any other medium, and a good hard look at directory ads, programs, and controls will pay off for many shoestring marketers.

BUYERS SEEKING SELLERS

Your salespeople and marketing programs seek out buyers. But buyers also seek sellers. Engineers, purchasing agents, and other buyers look for products and services to meet new needs, for companies that sell these products, and for local sales representatives.

When buyers search for sellers, they may use a pre-file catalog, a collection of product catalogs from different manufacturers. Although directories and pre-file catalogs sometimes are grouped together as "annuals," they are different. A directory is like a dictionary, while a pre-file catalog is like an encyclopedia.

Buyers go to a pre-file catalog to get specs and information on products; they go to a directory to find out where to call or write. A directory usually covers many more companies, but offers less information on each firm. Directories usually cover a broader field than a pre-file catalog. Typical directories are telephone Yellow Pages and the *Thomas Register of American Manufacturers*. A typical pre-file catalog is the *Chemical Engineering Catalog*.

Where else will a buyer turn to get information?

☐ Business directories
☐ Literature on hand
☐ Calls from salespeople
☐ Periodicals and direct mail
☐ Recommendations

Yearly Review

Once a year, you should examine your company's directory program. The most logical time is when you approve its single largest directory contract. At that time, look at all your directory efforts. Gather up the contracts for your national advertising, local advertising, and cooperative advertising. Know what you and your representatives are spending.

Then you are ready to set objectives for your overall program. Your objective may be to:

☐ Alert prospects who are hunting for your product.

☐ Compete for market share.

☐ Increase contacts for local offices or representatives.

When you set objectives, consider each product or service separately. Even the best known international company has new products, undersold or neglected products, and underused sales outlets.

Consider all relevant directories and buyer assistance avenues. Narrow your choices to only directories that could help prospects find your products. You will come up with a combination of Yellow Pages, local and national industrial directories, and specialized directories.

Beware of sacred cows. Directory programs should be balanced and coordinated. No single directory or family of directories is used by everyone in every market for every product or service. Determine to whom (title, industry, geographical area) you want to provide information. Determine which publications those prospects read for the type of information you're providing, based on directory subjects, circulation analysis, user preference studies, and monitored results. Make sure that you consider all directories fairly. Don't overlook the specialized directories and buyers' guides that zero in on your market.

Enhancing Aided Recall

Ideally, your company's products and sales outlets should be listed in every directory that looks useful under each heading into which your company falls. Deciding where to advertise will be the most time consuming part of your planning. When a buyer looks for a seller, you want to have the advantage of aided recall over unaided recall. When they use a directory to select sellers to contact, buyers seem to be influenced by two factors: the reputation of the companies they see listed as suppliers and the extra information suppliers offer through directory advertising.

Get your name listed everywhere it should and can be within each directory. It is important to know the listing policy and fees of every directory in which you are interested. Listing policies are more lenient in the industrial and specialized business directories. The policies often are not published. You must get details from the sales representative.

Next, look at sales results from your current directory advertising, including new business, present repeat business, and expected repeat business. You also should make sure that you've determined sales objectives. A directory program should get results. Every decision (which directory, headings, advertising level) should be based on its expected return. For a given amount of advertising, which combination of directory programs gives the greatest return?

You never will have enough information to answer that question precisely, but you should approach your decisions with those factors in mind.

Rules for Directory Programs

Here are a few rules to remember as you set up a directory program.

1. Directories are a poor way of keeping your name in front of people, because the ads are seen by relatively few readers. But those readers do read the ads carefully.
2. Consider your whole directory program. Balance your investments against results.
3. Expect to spend time on details.
4. Design your advertising specifically for each directory.

Business advertisers will find that selecting directories in the next few years will be complicated by head-to-head competition among directory publishers. Still, buyers have been slow to abandon an established directory for a new one that gives the same coverage and information. Advertisers must determine whether a directory is doing an adequate job or whether it is vulnerable to competition.

Circulation audits are available from the *Thomas Register, U.S. Industrial Directory, MacRae's,* and several of the Thomas Regional Guides. Unaudited circulation data are available from *Contractors Register, Ameritech Industrial Yellow Pages* and *BellSouth Industrial Pages.* Most buyers' guides published in conjunction with business publications provide detailed circulation information.

A REVIEW OF MAJOR DIRECTORIES

Here's a brief review of some of the major directories. Because they are national in scope, some current cost information is provided:

Business-to-Business Yellow Pages. About $110 million of Yellow Pages advertising is placed in the 21 business-to-business editions that have developed in metropolitan areas over the past 10 years (see Figure 7-1). Those editions go to business phone locations and carry headings of interest to businesses. Using northern New Jersey as an example, typical unit circulation is:

- □ Wholesale, retail, customer service—65%
- □ Manufacturers—12%
- □ Financial & real estate—11%
- □ Business services—5%
- □ Transportation & utilities—5%
- □ Farms—1%

Rates in business to business directories are comparable to or higher than rates in consumer Yellow Pages. A quarter-column ad varies from $1152 to $3102. Circulations typically are about 30% of the circulations of corresponding consumer Yellow Pages, or from 178,000 to 702,000.

The first business-to-business directory appeared in Chicago. Following that, 23 others were started in other metropolitan areas. Of those, five were discontinued, two merged, and two more are scheduled to be dropped. Advertising in the remaining directories is stable.

Regional Business Directories

NEW ENGLAND

Connecticut B-B YP
Eastern Massachusetts B-B YP
Eastern New England Guide
(Thomas Regional)
New England Industrial YP
(Ameritech)
Rhode Island—Southeastern Mass
B-B YP
Western New England Guide
(Thomas Regional)

MID-ATLANTIC

Contractors Register (NY-NJ-CT)
Eastern Pennsylvania Industrial YP
(Ameritech)
Greater Allegheny Guide (Thomas
Regional)
Greater Delaware Valley Guide
(Thomas Regional)
Greater Pittsburgh B-B YP
Greater New York Guide (Thomas
Regional)
New York County B-B YP
New York-New Jersey Industrial
YP (Ameritech)
North Jersey B-B YP
North Jersey Guide (Thomas
Regional)
Philadelphia-Greater Delaware
Valley B-B YP
Regional Industrial
Pages—Mid-Atlantic Edition
(BellSouth)
Western/Central New York Guide
(Thomas Regional)
Western Pennsylvania-Western NY
Industrial YP (Ameritech)

SOUTHEAST

Capital Cities Guide (Thomas
Regional)
Contractors Register
(Baltimore-Washington-Philadelphia)
Contractors Register (Florida)
Regional Industrial Pages—Florida
Edition (BellSouth)
Regional Industrial
Pages—Georgia-Alabama–Mid-East
Tennessee (BellSouth)

Greater Baltimore B-B YP
Regional Industrial
Pages—Mid-Atlantic Edition
(BellSouth)
Regional Industrial Pages—North
& South Carolina Edition (BellSouth)

MIDWEST

CBT B-B YP (Southwestern Ohio)
(Donnelley)
Chicago B-B YP
Cleveland & NE Ohio B-B YP
Dayton-Cincinnati-Southeastern
Ohio B-B YP (Ameritech)
Greater Michigan Guide (Thomas
Regional)
Greater Milwaukee B-B YP
Illinois Industrial YP (Ameritech)
Indiana Central B-B YP
Indiana Industrial YP (Ameritech)
Michigan Industrial YP (Ameritech)
Minneapolis-St. Paul B-B
North Central Tristate Guide
(Thomas Regional)
Northern Ohio Guide (Thomas
Regional)
Ohio Industrial YP (Ameritech)
Ohio Valley Guide (Thomas
Regional)

SOUTHWEST

Regional Industrial Pages-Gulf
Coast Edition (BellSouth)
North Texas-Oklahoma Guide
(Thomas Regional)

WEST

Contractors Register (California)
Business Buyers Guide North
(Pacific Bell)
Los Angeles B-B YP
Orange County B-B YP (California)
Regional Industrial Pages:
Washington Oregon Edition
(BellSouth)

B-B YP: *Business-to-Business
Yellow Pages*
    *All yellow pages sold by local
yellow page representatives unless
otherwise noted.*

Figure 7-1. Regional business directories can be a good way to reach business
customers for your products or services.

105

Yellow Pages. There are about 6000 Yellow Pages directories in the United States. Of the $6 billion total annual ad revenue that those directories earn, at least $200 million comes from business- or industry-oriented advertising. Typical advertisers are small manufacturers with local business markets, representatives, and distributors. National advertisers show distributors, reps, and sales offices under trademark and trade name advertising. Business advertising is concentrated in metropolitan area Yellow Pages and in business-to-business directories.

National Industrial Directories. Three broad national directories—*Thomas Register of American Manufacturers, U.S. Industrial Directories,* and *MacRae's Blue Book*—carry $55 million in advertisements from 17,000 advertisers. Approximately 90% of those ads appear in the *Thomas Register,* which has 40,000 headings compared to 3000 categories in a typical business-to-business Yellow Pages.

The directories cover the country with relatively small circulations. The *Thomas Register* has 55,000 paid subscriptions. Circulation for the other two publications is mostly controlled: 13% of the 35,000 circulation for the *U.S. Industrial Directory* and 9% of the 25,000 for *MacRae's* are paid.

The typical directory is kept for several years and used by a number of buyers, mainly in industrial purchasing, engineering, and production. A two and one half inch by one inch column ad (comparable to a Yellow Page quarter-column) costs about $800 on a one-time basis. The fee for a full page is about $3200.

Regional Industrial Directories. Four companies now publish these directories with a total of about $28 million in advertising. In order of seniority, they are:

1. *Contractors Register.* Publishes directories in the New York City area, Philadelphia, Washington, Baltimore, Florida, and California. Each lists contractors and their suppliers in the area. Circulation 30,000 to 40,000, mainly contractors; 12% are purchasing agents and engineers in industry and government who hire contractors. Minimum charge for an advertising program is $465; a quarter page costs $560.

2. *Thomas Regional Industrial Purchasing Guide Series.* In addition to its national register, Thomas publishes 14 guides in the Northeast, Midwest, and Southwest that list local suppliers of products and services bought by industry and government—circulation 20,000 to 35,000, read by purchasing agents, engineers, and management. Five directories have circulation audits and are largely request circulation. In the series' minimum ad program, a typical quarter-column ad runs about $1200 on a one-time basis. Full page is about $2500.

3. *Ameritech Industrial Yellow Pages.* In 1985, Midwest Bell bought the classified buying directory business. Directories are compiled for Illinois-Wisconsin, Indiana, Michigan, and Ohio. Ameritech plans directories for New England, New York-New Jersey, the Philadelphia area, and Pittsburgh to Buffalo. The Ameritech directories have the same editorial and circulation objectives as the Thomas regional directories. Ameritech guarantees a circulation larger than the comparable Thomas regional publications, but it does not provide audited circulation results.

4. *BellSouth Industrial Pages.* Bell in the Southeast offers industrial directories for Florida, Georgia-Alabama-Mid-East Tennessee, North and South Carolina, and Virginia-West Virginia-Maryland-Delaware. It plans to produce three more for the Gulf Coast, Northeast Texas, and Oregon-Washington. Circulations are similar to those of Ameritech industrial directories and larger than the circulation of comparable Thomas regionals, with no details provided.

Both the Ameritech and the BellSouth directories are part of the National Yellow Pages Service Association (NYPSA), and can be used by members. The Thomas Regional Directories are not part of the association.

Specialized Directories. Many specialized directories serve specific fields. Many are special issues of periodicals. An example is the Buyer's Guide issue of *Chemical Week*. Others, like the *Plant Engineering Directory and Specifications Catalog,* are closely connected to periodicals but sold separately. The rates and circulations for specialized directories are comparable to business periodicals in each field.

Addresses of Directory Publishers

Ameritech Industrial Yellow Pages
35 W. Huron Street, Suite 700
Pontiac, MI 48058
313-334-4100

BellSouth National Publishing
2635 Century Parkway N.E., Suite 850
Atlanta, GA 30345
800-348-4884

Contractors Register
30 Undercliff Avenue
Elmsford, NY 10523
914-592-8200

MacRae's Industrial Directory
817 Broadway
New York, NY 10003
212-673-4700

National Yellow Page Service Association
888 W. Big Beaver Road, Suite 414
Troy, MI 48048
313-362-3300

Thomas Regional Directory Co.
330 W. 34th Street
New York, NY 10001
212-290-7390

Thomas Register
One Penn Plaza
New York, NY 10019
212-695-0500

U.S. Industrial Directory
8 Stamford Forum
P.O. Box 10277
Stamford, CT 06904
203-328-2500

DESIGNING DIRECTORY ADS

The design for directory ad programs should be separate from other types of ads you might run, say, in a local paper or a trade newsletter. Because a directory user immediately searches for a specific heading, the advertisement does not need great stopping power. A directory ad should cover every possible reason for the user to contact the advertiser.

Directory users are interested in what you have to sell and they want to read about it. Your ad should cover only the product or service included in the heading. If you sell tires and molded rubber parts, design separate ads for each. The reader who looks up molded rubber parts is unlikely to be simultaneously interested in tires.

In industrial directories, the best rule is to advertise under the most specific headings possible. For example, you would choose the *Relays: Timing* heading, rather than *Electrical Equipment*. Prospects look up specific product headings first. Run several ads under specific headings instead of a larger ad under an umbrella heading.

Audience Specific Ads

In most cases, an ad should be designed specifically for the directory in which it appears. If the audience consists of purchasing agents, emphasize buying information and contacts. Design engineers are most interested in information on products. Plant engineers want to know where they can get a specific brand or size for immediate replacement.

To write your ads, first answer this question: Given the competitors listed under this heading, why should any buyer contact me? Draft a thorough list of all sales points, and incorporate these points into the copy. A prospective buyer needs only one reason to call. Catch the greatest possible number of prospects by including the maximum number of reasons in your ad.

The rules here differ greatly from what's necessary for other display ads or brochures. When you design your ads, remember that white space and attractive illustrations are not as important as good information. Copy should be readable. Avoid a variety of type sizes and styles. Only use illustrations that sell. Avoid plant shots, pictures, and stylized company names. Distributors and representatives, should use logos rather than just names.

Headlines should give reasons to call. However, your company's name, address, and telephone number can be in smaller print and at the bottom of the ad. Prospects who decide to call will find that information.

Three factors that affect the cost of all directory programs are ad size, placement, and color.

- ☐ **Ad size.** There is some indication that ad size increases response, at least with buyers who are not familiar with the products advertised. The larger the ad, the greater the result, given that the ad has a full complement of information and reasons for buying.

- ☐ **Ad placement.** Yellow Page publishers say that if you get placed ahead of competitors, you'll get more calls. That may be true with some consumer products that are purchased without extended consideration. But business buyers are more likely to consider all vendors listed under a heading, regardless of where the ad is placed.

- ☐ **Color.** Red ink has been added to directories. Red ads attract the eye and get faster recognition. Is color worth the money? No one knows yet.

If You Have Several Offices

Many industries advertisers use the alphabetical sections of the *Thomas Register, U.S. Industrial* and *MacRae's* directories to list local representatives and sales offices. Some companies use corporate profile ads to list names and phone numbers of corporate personnel, local representatives, or sales offices. However, the long life of the directories poses a problem for the method. Lists of representatives tend to be outdated pretty rapidly and are therefore useless.

Other national advertisers allow sales offices to do their own local directory advertising, using Yellow Pages or regional industrial directories.

An alternative is to use toll-free numbers, with a central operator to tell prospects where the outlet in their area is located. One advantage of a toll-free number is that distributor referrals are up-to-date.

Tracking Results

Because the purpose of directory advertising is to attract customers and prospects, it is absolutely essential to track results.

You cannot depend on salespeople or telephone operators to monitor calls. Without a monitoring system, a directory advertiser usually cannot determine of where calls come from. They could be from:

☐ Former customers who were reminded to call by directory advertising.

☐ Present customers who weren't aware you provided a product until they saw your directory listing.

☐ New people at existing or former customer companies who did not hear about you from the people they replaced.

☐ Prospects you've visited, who were reminded to call you by directory ads or listings.

There are four major methods you can use to monitor directory contacts.

1. For years, marketers have used **key addresses** to track mail responses. The easiest way is to use street numbers one or two digits off the regular number. Using department numbers in addresses is less reliable but still effective. As more inquiries are done by phone, key addresses can no longer check full response for most advertisers.

2. **Dedicated key phones** answered internally or by an answering service are effective but expensive in checking phone response. You know who called, for what, and when. The costs are for the phone line and labor.

3. **Remote call forwarding**— in which calls go to a number that is a short toll call away from the advertising office—is a productive compromise. Calls are automatically routed to the regular switchboard without interruption. The advertiser gets a bill each month with the time and date of each call. The cost is about $30 a month, plus 15 or 20 cents a call. The number of calls received is exact, although callers are not identified.

4. Finally, you can encourage response through your **toll-free number**. However, the system itself cannot check the number and source of calls, except by totalling the time length of incoming calls. But you can connect the toll-free number to a dedicated key phone and record who called, for what, and when.

Here to Stay and Getting More Popular

Advertising in business directories is a wave of the future. The directories continue to grow in popularity and are becoming available in other forms, such as on-line. As a reasonably low-cost marketing technique to reach a highly targeted market, they merit strong consideration.

8

CREATING AN UNFORGETTABLE BROCHURE

It ain't bragging if you really done it.

Dizzy Dean

Practically every business needs written literature to alert potential clients of products and services, and to display an image that attracts business. The brochure is one such vehicle—a handy and succinct way to market in print. The brochure provides ample space to attract attention through creative graphics, inform readers about your business, and impress them with your capabilities. It can be mass mailed, handed out, or enclosed with personal letters. If it is impressive enough, it may even be handed from one potential client to another. The best brochures have a fairly long "shelf life." They do not become outdated after a few months or even a year off the press, and they can be kept by clients as a reminder of your business.

Because of the multitude of purposes and uses served by the brochure, it is an item where skimping does not pay. You will need to spend more money here than on many other marketing activities, but the pay-off is also likely to be greater. What you should aim for is not necessarily the least expensive brochure you can obtain, but the most cost effective one.

YOU ARE WHAT THEY READ

For many businesses, especially professional service providers, the first exposure to the potential client is in print. They may hear about you and then call for more information, which you send, or they may receive your literature unsolicited or from a friend or colleague. The image created by your literature is their first, and often lasting, impression of you and your ability to provide what they need. You may be a new, small firm in a windowless low-rent office, but high quality literature can create the impression of an established powerhouse firm.

When architects John Diller and Peter Shaddock left a large firm to start their own architectural business, they created their brochure before they had their first client and while working out of their homes. Their eye-catching but not very expensive idea was to print the brochure in the same blue and white colors and same thin-line typeface used in architects' blueprints. Their graphics were renderings of their own homes, which each had designed several years before, but without any labeling that identified these as "my house." Along with a description of their qualifications and services, the brochure created an impression of high creativity and quality—exactly the characteristics that architects' clients tend to seek.

Paper Sells

The business world is replete with cases where brochures have generated business that wouldn't otherwise have surfaced, and given these cases, it doesn't take a very sophisticated analysis to determine that the dollars spent on a brochure can come back to you many times over.

Examples of this immediate cost effectiveness are found frequently among small companies that need to generate business outside their immediate geographic area, such as a small supplier of horse care products whose purchasers might be horse owners in any part of the country. Such companies cannot rely on a national sales force to make face-to-face calls, and national advertising is prohibitively expensive. Instead, these entrepreneurs rely heavily on quality brochures mailed to a target audience. Time and time again, without visiting the office or listening to a sales pitch, clients and customers order products or commit to services on the strength of the brochure they receive.

Cathy Bellizzi and Mona Piontkowski, both of Seminar Information Service, Inc., in Irvine, California, offer this advice to potential seminar attendees who receive a brochure in the mail: "A haphazard, gaudy brochure heralds a haphazard, unfocused seminar. A clean, informative, concise brochure indicates that more thought and planning went into it—and time spent on a quality brochure usually means time spent on a quality seminar." They also caution that "extraordinarily ornate brochures can be a signal that the seminar givers are not completely secure in their knowledge, so they make up for it by overdoing the mailing piece."

Produce a brochure with clarity, quality, and completeness, but don't overdo it. The *look* of the brochure should reflect what you want its reader to *feel* about your business, product, and/or services. The *content* of the brochure should reflect what you want readers to *know and understand* about your business, products, and/or services. Use the following checklist to make sure your brochure reflects these factors.

Outside. The cover of the brochure should announce your business name (or the name of products/services offered) and a brief description. For example, "Jensen Communications: For full service advertising and public relations campaigns." Or, "Time To Count On—A two-day time management seminar for corporate executives." The latter example also needs to include the name of the sponsoring firm somewhere on the cover. A handsome graphic or company logo can help the cover to appear professional and interesting.

In most cases, the cover is a poor place to attempt to be humorous or cute. Busy people want to know right away what they can expect when they open the brochure. They don't want brochures that announce "Open This At Your Own Risk" or "Psst . . . We've Got An Important Message for You."

Inside.   Be concise when describing your business, products, or services. Avoid any long, narrative statements that leave the reader wondering what you are offering. Instead, immediately address who, what, where, why, and when. The text may include:

A general "capabilities statement" about what you can do and who can use your services.

Specific achievements. If you are a new company without a track record, use specific examples of the kind of work you are prepared to do, such as earth moving for small and large sites of any slope; clearing and stump removal; excavation in preparation for concrete slab; engineering construction of earth retaining systems.

Quotes from satisfied clients and customers. If you don't have any in writing, request comments from existing clients. Potential customers want to know that you come highly recommended.

Event dates and places, if applicable, such as in the case of brochures about upcoming seminars.

Price information, if applicable. You don't want to "box yourself in" if you are in a business where price could vary. But, if you are marketing fixed-price items or services, by all means include the price.

Mail-in form or card. Forms for placing orders, attending events, or requesting more information can be a very effective way of immediately "closing the sale," or at least moving closer toward it. You can insert a separate card or use one leaf of the brochure with cut-on-the-dotted-line instructions.

Biographies of key personnel. Use brief biographical sketches of the key people in your firm or those who will be directly providing the services offered. Include their educational backgrounds and experience pertinent to the services offered.

Added attractions. If there are any additional "pluses" that your company offers that might make it stand out from others, mention them briefly. For example, a moving company might mention guaranteed delivery dates or an accounting firm might state that weekend appointments are available.

Name, address, phone number. Place these prominently. Most readers will look for them on the front or back cover of the brochure.

DESKTOP PUBLISHING

If you have desktop publishing capabilities, you can experience substantial savings in developing your brochure and these other marketing supporting vehicles. Desktop publishing enables you to draft your content, reduce it to size, combine a variety of typefaces and sizes, produce layouts and mock-ups, incorporate graphics, and take other steps previously reserved for professionals in the graphic, layout, and printing business. You simply determine the parameters, such as size of the brochure and number of folds (see Figure 8-1), incorporate it into your program, and you'll get to see it all on the computer screen as you work.

With desktop publishing you can experiment with larger or bolder type, horizontal vs. vertical layout, etc. To produce "camera-ready" copy for quantity printing, however, you will need a top quality printer compatible with your computer—at least letter or laser print quality rather than dot matrix.

Figure 8-1. There are many different brochure formats to choose from, depending on the number of words and pictures you need to show and the amount of money you can spend.

GRAPHICS WITHOUT GRIEF

Many small business entrepreneurs shy away from even attempting a high quality brochure because they feel it will require expensive artwork that can only be created by a high-priced graphic artist. It is true that good graphics can make a brochure, while poorly conceived graphics can break it. However, graphics don't have to be elaborate to demonstrate quality. Many excellent brochures effectively use the company's logo as the primary graphic, sometimes repeated in several places throughout the printed material.

Big businesses spend substantial time and money in the creation of an effective, eye-catching logo. Art directors labor over ideas and submit a few of the best. Marketing personnel test the concepts on typical consumers. Managers meet to mull over the designs and send them back for redesign. Finally, a design is conceived that meets with wide approval and will represent the business for years to come. The price tag is hefty.

If you can't afford to hire an ad agency for logo design and test marketing, you can still come up with a concept that can be drafted—often right in a print shop—into an effective logo for your business. One of the best ways to do this is to develop a logo from word graphics, using the name or initials of your business creatively.

One ad agency design director describes the idea of word graphics in this way: "The challenge is to make a good name operate at its highest level of effectiveness by presenting it with graphic excellence. The basic requirements for the relationship between name and design apply across the board: readability, memorability, and optimum image connotations."

Start leafing through magazines to find logos developed from word graphics. You'll be amazed at how many you recognize (see Figure 8-2). Often, it takes only a graphic presentation of one or two letters, rather than the entire business name. The "M" in McDonald's echoes the familiar golden arches. The "K" encompasses the Kodak name in a square. The Volkswagen logo is so well identified with the product that we have to look at it twice to remember it is simply the "V" and "W" handsomely presented in a circle.

McDonald's trademark

Volkswagen's trademark

Kodak's trademark

SpaghettiO's trademark

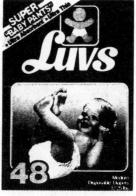

Procter & Gamble's trademark

Playskool's trademark

Johnson & Johnson's trademark

IBM's trademark

Express Mail's trademark

Figure 8-2. These simple yet well-known logos illustrate how attractive and expressive well-designed letter forms can be. Logos reprinted with permission.

In an effective departure on this theme, Spaghettios singles out the "O" by printing it larger and in red, appropriately reminding us of the "O" shaped noodles found in the can.

When you look at other word graphic logos, notice how different typefaces are used to create a variety of images. A highly personal image is created when type appears handwritten, as in the logos for Luvs Diapers and Johnson & Johnson. These products are for personal home use, and their word graphics remind us of that fact.

When a logo is to be associated with a more playful product, it can use more playful lettering, such as the elementary cut-out look created for Playskool Toys.

Business products, on the other hand, typically use typefaces that are bold and vertical. The essential element is image. Letters themselves can suggest elegance, youth, age, fun, reliability, or creativity. If you think about the image you want to project, you can probably find a way to depict it with a typeface.

Many word graphic logos have even managed to give an impression of the product or service itself. Express Mail puts its image into print by leaning the letters of its name to the right and incorporating bold underlining. IBM uses its initials as a word graphic that reminds us of contemporary computer output.

To turn your company's name into an effective word graphic logo, start by doodling. Write the full name, then the initials, then just the first letter. Write these horizontally, vertically, and diagonally. Try some overlapping and intertwining of the letters. Write block letters and letters leaning to the right or to the left. Encompass them in circles, squares, and triangles. Think about the image you want to portray, and look at logos that portray a similar image. When you develop something you like, you probably will need a graphic artist to fine-tune the concept. But you won't need an entire advertising agency to start from scratch and bill you accordingly.

THE BROCHURE SCAN

One of the best ways to develop ideas for your own brochure is to start collecting others—those in unrelated fields for general look and content as well as those in your own area of business. Select those you feel are particularly noteworthy and begin thinking of ways you can make yours even better. Ask yourself:

□ Which elements create an image of a firm I would want to do business with? The client list? The quotes from satisfied customers? The biographies of top personnel?

□ How do they explain what they do without being overly wordy? Do they list examples? Do they limit themselves to a few well-chosen sentences and phrases? Do they use drawings or photos? Do they use glowing adjectives like *most, value, best, experienced,* and *finest*? Can I incorporate some of these specific words and phrases into my brochure?

□ What is the order of content—elements such as name and address, personnel biographies, capabilities overview, and client quotes?

□ Which devices make the layout interesting? Generous white space around print? Various sizes of type? Boldface and underlining?

□ How many words are contained in those brochures that seem to give adequate information without being wordy?

□ Does color make a difference? Which colors seem most appealing?

□ Does the paper quality make a difference?

□ How do graphics and artwork help create an image? How much space do they take up? Are they simple or fancy?

□ What is it about the front cover that grabs my attention?

After you have examined numerous brochures and determined their best qualities, you should have plenty of ideas for drafting your own content and rough layout. First, draft the content. Count words, compare them to the word count in the best brochures you've scanned, and cut as necessary. Then, decide where you want your various content elements to appear and where you want to use graphics. Use graph paper to cut and paste a mock-up of your brochure, penciling in areas that represent blocks of content and graphics.

At this point, you need the services of professionals—a graphic artist who can take your rough ideas and put them into camera-ready form, as well as a full service print shop that can determine whether your copy and graphics will fit as you have estimated. Professional artists and printers can:

☐ Develop camera-ready graphics

☐ Assist with selection of paper and ink

☐ Assist with decisions about typeface and sizes

☐ Determine the need for cutting or adding to your content

☐ Lay out all elements in final size so you'll see how they look together

☐ Set type (which you'll need to proof for errors)

☐ Produce a mock-up that incorporates content and graphics for final revision

☐ Print

☐ Fold

Unfortunately, you can't afford to cut corners on these professional services—nor would you want to. The production of final graphics, the typesetting, and the final printing can make the difference between a brochure that looks "quick and dirty" and one that has enough quality to bring you a fairly immediate return on your investment.

The Brochure That Nobody Throws Away

If your brochure is truly excellent, it has a chance of remaining in the files and on the desks of those who receive it. They may keep it because they like its style or because they suspect they may need to refer to its content again and again.

Tony Alessandra, who conducts management seminars and delivers speeches to corporations nationwide, developed such a brochure to market his services. Produced on heavy, glossy cardboard weight paper stock, the Alessandra "brochure" is actually a 9 by 11 inch file folder that one might use for organizing and carrying papers.

The brochure creates an image of high quality and eye appeal. The cover is royal purple, and at the very bottom, in shiny gold, are Alessandra's name, address, and phone number (including an 800 number, which immediately signifies that he is a "heavy hitter" in his profession). Inside, Alessandra does not describe his business early in the brochure as is traditional. Instead, he fills the space with impressive quotes from satisfied clients, separated by plenty of white space and bordered by two dynamic photographs of Alessandra on the speaker's platform. When the folder is opened, it becomes a colorful poster displaying books, pamphlets, and videotapes by Alessandra, surrounded by one-paragraph descriptions of each.

When we examine the content, we find the creation of an image, rather than a step-by-step description of what he can do for you. For example, the back cover of this file folder brochure says nothing about Alessandra or what he does. Instead, it builds his image by noting:

> As the room lights dim, a hush comes over the audience in anticipation of the keynote address. "Ladies and gentlemen, Dr. Tony Alessandra," echoes the announcer as the energetic figure walks briskly onto the stage. Departing from tradition, he passes the awaiting podium, steps off the stage and directly into the audience. He delivers his first line and the hush in the room is broken with spontaneous laughter and applause. From that moment on, the electricity of Tony Alessandra never stops.

In general, the brochures that are not easily thrown away are creative in their content, attractive, and printed on quality paper. The price tag may be more than some other marketing tools you will use, but the ability of the brochure to attract business over time produces a cost effective return on investment.

Trade Associations and Your Brochure

You probably are a member of an association that represents your area of business. Chances are your business is represented by more than one such association. Associations exist for almost every imaginable business, ranging from the Building Service Contractor Association to the American Institute of CPAs. At the very least, you'll want to list your association memberships in your brochure, giving your business a serious, professional image.

Your professional associations also may supply a brochure for its members. You've probably received these from an insurance or real estate agent. These brochures contain *boilerplate* material about the products or services, and leave a blank back cover or white space for a printed label to be attached with your specific company's information. This is a shoestring marketer's dream because it gives you an excellent opportunity to acquire quality literature for a much smaller investment than would be required if you started from scratch.

Some associations have general consumer education literature pertinent to the field in the forms of file card handouts, pamphlets, or press releases. Subject matter may range from how to organize your tax information throughout the year to how to teach your children to brush their teeth. These may be acquired or copied for inclusion in your brochure. Since they contain educational materials, they help make your brochure the kind of reference source that people will remember.

Professional organizations typically have codes of ethics, codes of conduct, mottos, or other written devices that form principles for members to adhere to. Your use of these as a starting point in designing your literature creates a high standard for your own firm and an image of professional excellence.

Stock Photo Companies

You've decided to produce a brochure for your accounting business. The text and graphics are laid out and ready for the camera, but you haven't come up with a cover photo yet. The theme of the pamphlet is "Saving Your Pennies." You decided that a cover photo of shiny, new pennies is needed. You consider yourself a pretty good amateur photographer, so you pull out the close-up lens and put a white backing on your desk against the wall. You stack up new pennies and take a few shots. Perfect. You send them out to be developed.

When the pictures come back, however, you aren't impressed. To get the vivid colors and contrasts that catch a customer's eye, you must know what you are doing. Flip open a colorful magazine like *Time, Fortune,* or *People.* Look at their pictures. They're very good and succeed in catching your eye. This is the quality you need in order to complete your brochure. However, these shots were taken by people whose livelihood is photography. Moral: If you want it done well, hire people who know what they're doing. Good photographers are very expensive. For a custom photo of you, your office, or your staff, however, you may not have much choice. A good photographer can give you exactly what you need and usually pretty quickly.

Professional photographer's prices generally are based on the final usage. For instance, if you just want a few shots to frame and place around your office, a photographer may not ask much. But if your glossy flyer is going to saturate a major metropolitan area, that is another story. The copyright laws protect the originators of the photos. The photographer owns the rights to the photo unless specifically indicated otherwise in a contract.

However, you still need a quality photo of a pile of shiny pennies, and you don't want to pay a lot. What can you do?

The answer is stock photos or, for a different type of picture, public domain photos. Stock photo houses are agencies that keep anywhere from thousands to millions of negatives in stock. Virtually every conceivable picture has been taken and stored for use by anyone who needs a picture.

Suppose you want a picture of the *Queen Mary* for your travel agency brochure. For a price, stock photo companies will happily provide what you need. A stock photo firm is a photo library, stocking its files with photographs of many subjects or perhaps one subject. Most stock houses sell a photo for a one-time use or, more precisely, sell the reproduction rights of the photo for a one-time use. The photo, usually a color slide, is returned after it is color separated.

There are some restrictions on the handling of contracted photos. Color slides are delicate, easily scratched, and subject to damage from hot lights. Some stock photos may be a once-in-a-lifetime shot, which if scratched or damaged may be irreplaceable. Most stock firms specify that you may be charged a very high fee if you lose or damage an original slide.

Getting the stock photo is relatively easy if you know what you want. The firm will have a large catalog of the images on file, indexed so that you quickly can narrow down what you need. If you need the photo immediately, a firm can send a messenger with a slide you selected over the phone, but this kind of convenience is costly.

When you inquire about a photo, you will need to specify the following:

☐ description of the image you want

☐ black-and-white or color image

☐ type of use—editorial (magazines, books) or commercial (brochures, advertisements)

☐ when you need it

☐ amount and type of reproduction (determines pricing)

Cathy Sachs, of Woodfin Camp, Inc., a stock photo agency in Washington, DC, and public relations officer of the American Society of Picture Professionals says that stock photos are an excellent way to get exactly what you need quickly. But you pay for the convenience. Some stock photo houses are very expensive, with slides starting in the $700 range for one-time rights. Others can give you the ideal generic image you need to visually express your business for a mere $50! Sachs advises, however, that even a lofty price charged for a really spectacular negative may be more economical than settling for substandard advertising.

For the least expensive photo, she suggests trying large stock firms, whose volume business may keep the prices low, or the smaller firms off the beaten path, whose prices may remain at a level their customers can afford.

If you have decided that you need a stock photo, open up the yellow pages to "Photography—Stock Photos" and call around. See if the firm regularly handles needs like yours. If you are unsure of what you want, or you want a very specific image, be sure to inquire about any research fees, if applicable. Stock photos can be an excellent way to reduce the time or expense required for your marketing effort.

Public Domain Photos

Public domain photo collections are available free to the public or for a nominal reproduction fee. They are usually kept by libraries, government agencies, museums, and historical societies. These photographs are available for public use and are not reserved by copyright. The images in these banks include collections of nonprofit institutions, photos with expired copyrights, and any picture taken with taxpayers' money.

The advantage of public domain photos is that only a nominal duplication or printing fee is generally charged. The disadvantages include the time required to research large collections and the limited types of photos. A predominance of public domain photographs are historical.

Cathy Sachs observes that there is a "mindboggling" number of sources. If you are located near a major city, most libraries (public and private) have collections or information on area collections. The reference book *Picture Sources 3 and 4* (from the Special Libraries Association) lists public domain photo sources. Call (202) 234-4700 to order the book.

In rural areas, Sachs advises first calling area museums or libraries. If they can't give you the names of various collections, try state or county historical societies, the National Park Service, or a local Chamber of Commerce. Or, you could write to the American Society of Picture Professionals, Inc., Box 5283 Grand Central Station, New York, NY 10163-5283, an information clearinghouse for anyone involved or interested in photography or images.

Even the smallest town in the middle of nowhere may have public domain photo collections, according to Sachs. All you have to do is find them. Some of the rare shots provided could add an interesting and inexpensive twist to your marketing brochures and flyers.

BUSINESS CARDS AND PAPER NOVELTIES

Supplementary materials are vital to your marketing program. A dynamite brochure cannot be expected to overcome a poor image created by other literature distributed by your firm. This includes business cards, stationery (including envelopes), and flyers. Add to these an entire category called "paper novelties," such as calendars, memo pads, and other notions that bear your name.

Among these, your business card will be the most frequently used. You will enclose it with brochures (perhaps even developing a brochure that incorporates a special pocket or slits to hold your card) and hand it out on numerous occasions.

More Mileage from Business Cards

"Business cards are probably the most underused and least understood of all the basic sales resources," says Jonathan Evetts, president of Evetts Sales Seminars based in New York.

Every day, companies print and exchange hundreds of thousands of business cards, almost without a thought. Each time one of these unthinking transactions occurs, a valuable opportunity is lost, an opportunity to make the maximum impact with a permanent, accurate record of some very important information about yourself and your company.

"Properly used, your business card is almost like having your own miniature billboard," says Evetts, "and seen at arm's length, it is actually the same apparent size as a thirty-foot billboard viewed from a distance. If this seems like an exaggeration, remember that 'scaling up' your thinking about business cards in this way makes it easier to realize that your card probably contains more truly useful information than many full-sized billboards."

The card should, of course, show the company name, logo, address, and telephone number with its bearer's name and title.

Evetts observes, "Often we are rather careless in how we carry and present our cards. Cheap plastic cases are common, as are cards with corners bent from being kept in overfilled wallets. An extreme example of this occurred to a friend of mine, who was even asked to return a warped and grubby card that happened to have the family shopping list written on the back."

When exchanging business cards, it is worthwhile to extract the greatest advantage from the transaction. Begin to think of the card as an item of value, and then practice waiting for exactly the right moment to present one.

There is often a natural pause in the conversation with a prospect, somewhere at the start of the meeting, perhaps just after you have been asked to sit down. This can be the perfect time to take out your card. Evetts advises looking the prospect in the eye and, as you present it, repeating your name clearly and distinctly, even if you have introduced yourself only a few minutes earlier. This will leave an enduring impression of your appearance and your name, linked to that of your company and its logo.

"At this point," says Evetts, "if you are not offered a card in return, ask for one. Don't let the meeting proceed until the exchange of cards has been completed." But don't be embarrassed when someone doesn't happen to have a card. Instead, stress how important correct names and titles are to you, and ask for the information on a piece of paper.

"Far too many people never bother to ask for cards," Evetts says. "They just don't realize that they are missing a chance to show prospective customers that they care about details, and they forget that the most welcome words anyone can hear or see are his or her own name, properly pronounced and spelled."

Some Educational Examples

Although business cards generally come in one convenient size and cardboard stock, there are still plenty of options for design elements that make the difference between a business card that is distinctive and one that begs to be ignored. In Figure 8-3, you'll see a number of design elements that set some business cards well above the average:

A TOUR de force. The use of light line drawing as background for the print on this card makes us look twice—even three or four times—to decipher the bird's eye view of the Capitol. The use of a pale blue paper and traditional typefaces supports the image of elegance and professionalism.

Photo Studio. Immediately eye-catching is the geometric design of a lens shutter set in bold blue against white. An unusual, very vertical typeface helps to complete an image of high quality creativity—a very desirable image for a photographer to capture.

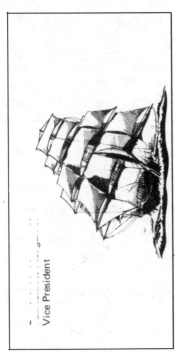

Vice President

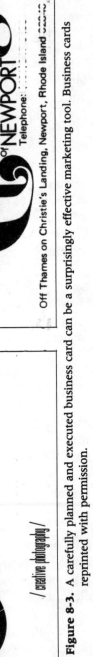

Off Thames on Christie's Landing, Newport, Rhode Island 02840. Business cards

Figure 8-3. A carefully planned and executed business card can be a surprisingly effective marketing tool. Business cards reprinted with permission.

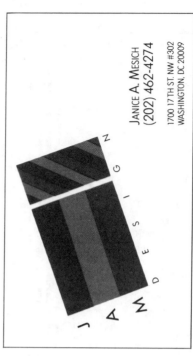

JANICE A. MESICH
(202) 462-4274

1700 17 TH ST. NW #302
WASHINGTON, DC 20009

THE FINEST AFLOAT

East Side of A1A — Hillsboro Inlet
Pompano Beach, Fla.

3 TRIPS DAILY
8 A.M. to 12 Noon and 1 to 5 P.M.
NIGHT TRIPS
7 P.M. to 11 P.M.
CHARTERS ON REQUEST
Weekend Bahama Trips
No Alcoholic Beverages Allowed
FUN FOR THE FAMILY

Pompano Beach
CAPT. - - - - - - - - Phone - - - - -

Figure 8-3. (continued)

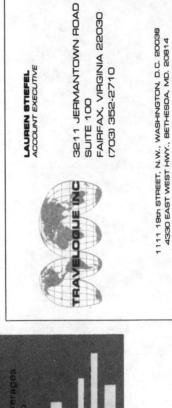

Figure 8-3. (continued)

Christie's of Newport. Using a fold-out business card, Christie's was able to use two good graphics that would have been too crowded on a standard size card. The tall ship graphic immediately reminds us of the finest traditions of the sea. It is highly appropriate for a fine restaurant in a seaside town. Inside, the distinctive large, bold lettering of "Christie's" catches our eye again.

Toscanini Ristorante. We know it's Italian the minute we glimpse the name and spelling. But, through the use of musical notes and violin graphics, we also get the image of Old World music as an important backdrop to dining. Music could have been mentioned, but it is more effectively implied visually on this card.

The Finest Afloat. There is probably no better way to present a boat ride than to show a gleaming white yacht under cloudless skies on a calm blue sea. This card uses both sides, letting the striking photograph create an image, and spelling out all necessary logistical details on the reverse side.

JAM Design. This card uses graphic excellence to get the message to potential clients about the design capabilities of the firm. The diagonal placement of the logo and the use of bold colors conveys creative flair. The result is an eye-catching business card with a message told by example.

Travelogue Inc. The use of a world map as background to the company name immediately invokes the image of a professional who sends clients anywhere in the world. Again, this message doesn't have to be stated; it is accomplished through graphics.

Canaan Valley Stores, Inc. The image created in this card is one of unblemished country, noted in the lakeside trees and big sky in the circular logo. The untraditional vertical element is distinctive.

The Skyline Clubs. The graphic depiction of a runner on this card immediately grabs attention. The repetition of the runner outline in three alternating colors expresses motion and, by implication, the fitness for which a health club should be noted. Because the graphic is so compelling, the remainder of the card is appropriately downplayed with a simple, clean typeface.

The Business Card They Can't Forget

While attending my first convention of the National Speakers Association, I was fortunate to meet Dr. Tony Alessandra and Dr. Michael LeBouef, both of whom were presenters at the convention.

Tony's business card, like his brochure, was unusual. On one side was the traditional message with phone number, address, and zip code much like anyone else's business card. On the other side, there was the replica of a silver coin with two hands shaking and the words "Building Sales" above and the words "Through Trust" below. Lower on the card was the title of Tony's book *Non-Manipulative Selling*, then his name, and the name of his co-author.

Tony's card was immediately appealing to me because it was an easy way to remind people of the name of your product or service—in his case, a book—without stopping and writing it out.

Michael LeBouef's business card also was unforgettable, featuring a picture of him seated on a large replica of his book *The Greatest Management Principles in the World* (New York: Putnam, 1985). Michael was seated in the lower right hand corner of the picture with his right hand "presenting" the book. Below his hand was his name, the three words "author," "lecturer" and "consultant," then his address and phone number. This very professionally produced card was in black and white.

After seeing these two cards, I decided that as a marketing author, I could indeed create a card that was powerful and memorable. In the coming weeks I worked with Doug Bushey of Profiles by Design in Fairfax, Virginia to establish what is now a classic among marketing innovations.

The card depicts me presenting my co-authored book *Marketing Your Consulting and Professional Services*. In the background is a set of shelves—really a photographer's screen that simulates an office atmosphere. My name, address, and phone number are in the upper lefthand corner of the card in white print. The print stands in mild contrast to the brilliantly colored card.

In the weeks that followed, I used the cards in all of my correspondence with editors and publishers, clients and prospects, and

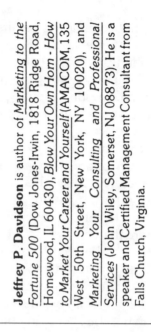

Jeffrey P. Davidson is author of *Marketing to the Fortune 500* (Dow Jones-Irwin, 1818 Ridge Road, Homewood, IL 60430), *Blow Your Own Horn - How to Market Your Career and Yourself* (AMACOM, 135 West 50th Street, New York, NY 10020), and *Marketing Your Consulting and Professional Services* (John Wiley, Somerset, NJ 08873). He is a speaker and Certified Management Consultant from Falls Church, Virginia.

Figure 8-4. Examples of cards that no one forgets. Reprinted with permission.

began to notice amazing results. Magazine editors began requesting copies of the book for review. Book publishers, to whom I was submitting new book proposals, seemed to be responding more quickly and were much more personable in phone conversation. Existing clients, prospective clients, friends and associates—everyone—found the card amusing, definitely memorable, and highly effective.

Since so much of our business and professional communication takes place by phone, the picture business card serves as a substitute for the "picture phone" that technology has long promised but not delivered. A person looking at your picture card in some sense feels more connected and in touch with you. To that person, you become much more than a voice; you become an individual with an image.

Although the picture business card costs more—not a shoestring marketing technique—the extra cost of the card more than pays for itself in very short order. And as an alternative to producing a more elaborate and expensive marketing tool, such as a brochure, it is just what the shoestring marketing doctor ordered.

9

STRATEGIC BULLETIN BOARDS

Wealth flows from energy and ideas.

William Feather

The essence of effective shoestring marketing is capturing the attention and interest of targeted prospects with effective, yet inexpensive vehicles. Whenever your message is professionally conveyed to targets, particularly with an absence of competition and other distracting messages, you are ahead of the game. I term placement of such messages *strategic bulletin boards*. These include action letters, building directories, office and library bulletin boards, directory listings, executive service plans, value packs, and specialized newsletters.

Each of these shoestring vehicles can be used and positioned in such a manner that you are providing a strategic bulletin board in the path of those whom you are trying to reach.

LET YOUR MAIL CARRIER DO THE WALKING

Scores of books and articles have been written about direct mail campaigns, and two examples are shown here. The optometrist has combined a geographically targeted letter (a bit on the long side) with a discount coupon (Figure 9-1). The automotive shop's card appears as a customer service rather than as a marketing ploy for more business (Figure 9-2).

Dear Neighbor,

Whether you have been in this neighborhood just a few weeks or a few years, we at Dr. Khalils office would like to introduce you to our practice.

One of the most difficult decisions you will have to make is finding an optometrist for you and your family. Without the advise of a trusted friend, you will be faced with choosing a name at random from the telephone directory or following a directory sign on the side of a building.

We are writing to help you make that decision in a way more in keeping with your expectation of high quality vision care.

We offer individual care for all members of your family. Our comprehensive optometric services include eye examinations, glacoma test, visual skills, retenal photography for detecting and document-ing retenal diseases, soft contact lenses for daily wear and extended wear, gas-permable contact lenses, astigmatic soft lenses and bifocal soft and hard lenses, large selection of fashionable eyeglass frames. We have the most modern equipment and we offer evening and Saturday hours.

We feel that you should be able to talk to the optometrist in person, to find out if his is the practice that you would feel comfortable with. The conversation should include an examination to determine the health of your eyes and your visual needs. With this in mind we would like to offer you the following *Introductory Welcoming Certificate*. In this way you may, at little cost to you, decide whether this is the practice for you.

Would you like more information please call 379-8898, and we will be happy to discuss any of your questions.

Warmest Regards,

Member
American Optometric Association

OPTOMETRIST

$10 OFF our complete (Reg. $40) eye exam
AND
$25 OFF the purchase of any complete pair of prescription eye glasses.
Large selection of frames available!

CONTACT LENSES
Many types and brands of lenses available at

20% off the Regular Price

• Family Discount Rate Available
• Glaucoma Testing
• Retinal Photography
• Bifocal Soft Lenses
• Gas Permeable Lenses
• Large Fashionable Frame Selection
• Lab On Premises

PLEASE CALL FOR APPOINTMENT

These Offers Valid With This Coupon Only

Figure 9-1. A direct mail piece used by a professional to generate awareness of and interest in his services.

138

AUTOMOBILE MAINTENANCE IS OUR PROFESSION

MALCOLM'S AUTOMOTIVE

4601 COLUMBIA PIKE
ARLINGTON, VIRGINIA 22204

According to our records it has been 90 days since your last Service and Maintenance check.

To help protect your investment, the Basic Preventive Maintenance will help keep your car in better condition and less chance of major repairs.

DON'T WAIT TOO LATE.
CALL NOW FOR AN APPOINTMENT!

MALCOLM'S AUTOMOTIVE

Figure 9-2. A mailing piece that helps produce follow-up business for an automobile service station.

The main problem with direct mail campaigns is cost. If you add up the costs of producing the promotional materials, acquiring the mailing labels and sending out the whole bunch, then having to repeat that process at least six more times—the experts recommend that the target be contacted at least seven times—the cost can be considerable. Moreover, there is considerable waste in the system, sometimes untraceable (i.e., mail going to those who don't want it, significant number of undelivered packages, and inadequate follow-up capabilities).

Action letters are a more rational method of reaching targets on an individual basis. They cost far less and can yield the same results as direct mail campaigns. I discuss action letters in *Marketing Your Consulting and Professional Services* (1985) and *Getting New Clients* (1987), both co-authored with Richard A. Connor, Jr. (New York: John Wiley & Sons).

How can action letters benefit retailers, distributors, and service providers?

Using various available directories (See Chapter 7), the local Yellow Pages, or existing customer files, choose ten targets to whom you will mail a personalized action letter. This carefully crafted letter on your president's stationery could:

☐ introduce your company and its products or services

☐ announce a new product or service

☐ discuss a special sale

☐ express your interest in making an appointment with the recipient.

This letter should be sent on a Monday if directed to local targets or sent on a Friday if directed to distant targets. The timing of these mailings ensures that the targets receive them by Wednesday or Thursday. Studies have shown that prospects are most receptive to new ideas and suggestions in the middle of the week and least receptive on Mondays and Fridays.

Why limit this mailing to ten? Certainly, with the advent of memory typewriters and word processors your company is capable of mailing out a far greater number. A limited mailing enables you to comfortably and effectively make an individualized personal follow-up. As the sample letter suggests (see Figure 9-3), you should close your letter by telling the prospect the date and time that you will call to discuss the message in the body of your letter. This is one of the most powerful strategic bulletin board techniques.

Even if your prospects toss the letter, as many will, when you call on the day and at the time that you said you would, you create a forum in which higher than usual receptivity can occur.

Your follow-up call should take place a week after the letter arrives, on a Tuesday, Wednesday, or Thursday. I have used this technique for three years and found it superior to, and less costly than any other method of prospecting.

Far too many marketers are willing to send out hundreds, if not thousands, of letters at once when there is really little or no possibility that any type of effective follow-up will be made. The shotgun process works well if you are selling items stored in your basement from a catalog. But for many small businesses, ten targeted letters (which quickly grow to 350 to 500 per year) does quite nicely.

Jeffrey P. Davidson, CMC
3709 S. George Mason Dr.
Falls Church, VA   22041
(703) 931-1984

January 10, 1988

Professor Irving Rein
Graduate School of Management
Northwestern University
Evanston, IL

Dear Professor Rein:

    I read High Visibility and found it to be a landmark book. As
a result of such a marvelous effort, I imagine you are inundated with
offers to speak across the country.

    I'm interested in your feedback to an idea which will relieve
some of the pressures of your busy schedule, while continuing to promote
High Visibility. As you know, I recently authored Blow Your Own Horn:
How to Market Yourself and Your Career (AMACOM Books). This book is
related to High Visibility because it instructs individuals on how to
gain more visibility to further their careers.

    I am willing and able to speak before a wide variety of groups and
on both radio and television as your replacement, when your schedule does
not permit your attendance. Naturally I would be speaking about my own
book, but as High Visibility is inextricably related, I would promote it
with equal fervor.

    I'll give you a call next Wednesday at 10:15 a.m., Central Time, to
discuss this further.

Yours truly,

Jeffrey P. Davidson

Figure 9-3. Action letter.

Putting on the Glitz

A variation on the theme of sending the targeted action letter is
to send a brief cassette message. I use three-minute cassettes and
tailor each message. Here is how it works.

First I find a local cassette tape distributor who can provide me with two-minute, three-minute, four-minute or any length of cassette tape that I require. Short cassettes work well in this procedure because the target who receives them immediately recognizes that the message on the tape is not long. Thus, odds that the target will pop it into a cassette machine, which virtually everyone has in their home, office, or car, is exceedingly high. The cassette distributor also provides blank labels at two cents each. On these labels I produce a custom message that reads, "A message for John Doe." Sometimes when I am in a hurry, I simply stamp my address on the cassette label and send it as is. In either case, the listening and retention ratio is amazingly high.

Working from a standard letter, I begin with the following script: "Dear Mr. XYZ, my name is Jeff Davidson and I'm the president of _____. The reason I am sending you this cassette message is because I believe my new _____ will greatly benefit your business. Recognizing that you are extremely busy, I will keep my message short and to the point."

I go on to give them two or three specific reasons why it is in their best interest to retain my services or buy the product I am offering. I repeat my address and phone number slowly and carefully. I conclude each message with "Thanks for your time and attention" or "Thanks for listening." I then say "Yours truly, Jeff Davidson" and put emphasis on my name as I close out the audio letter.

The results of this strategic "audio" board are quite impressive. I have had targets call me the very next day after receiving it, or they've written to me within a few days. The following week, when I call to discuss my service personally, I find that the retention rate is generally far greater than for a letter.

Even if they discard the tape immediately after listening to it, when I call, the connection is reestablished independent of whether or not I make a sale to that particular prospect. Most people don't get cassettes in the mail, at least not three minute ones. For this reason, my message is strategically positioned apart from, and hopefully superior to, the tons of print mail that busy executives receive each day.

The mechanics of producing ten cassette messages at a sitting are easier than you think. Since I only use one side of the three-minute cassette, the message is literally three minutes long. When I first pop it into the machine, I rewind it all the way to the beginning, then count eight seconds to make sure I have cleared the leader tape. I then begin simply with "Dear so and so" and proceed through with my presentation, making sure it does not sound canned or read.

If I stumble a tad here or there, I leave it in; it adds to the unique human quality of my presentation. If I make a large gaffe, the phone rings, or I am otherwise interrupted, I simply flip the switch to pause, break out of the record mode, back up a sentence and begin recording again by releasing the pause button. This makes only a minor blip in the finished recording.

Usually I am able to do an entire three-minute message without interruptions, but if I do have to stop on occasion, it is no problem. I routinely finish ten personalized cassette messages in under 45 minutes. Before sitting down for this taping session, I have already prepared the mailing package and any other inserts that will be included with the cassette. Then it is just a matter of finishing the cassette, rewinding it, inserting it in the envelope, and mailing it.

Voice has so many advantages over the printed word. Depending on what I am offering and to whom I am offering it, I will speak slowly and clearly in an authoritative voice, or cool and casual, or highly excited and enthused. Since your voice is uniquely yours, the prospects gain a sense of you that cannot be transmitted by a letter, even if you are a master of the printed word.

The Value Packs Are Here!

We all receive them in the mail: packages of coupons offering some type of discount from local product and service vendors. They are called *mail packs, discount packs,* or *value packs.* I have included them here because of the unique impact they can have among your target niche. Unlike mass marketed direct mail letters, participation in the value pack affords several key benefits:

☐ Your cost per target is considerably lower because your product or service offering is one of several contained in the package.

☐ Targets who receive and open the value packs report that they are likely to flip through the entire pack, pull out a couple of the coupons that may be of interest, then discard the rest. Thus, while traditional direct mail packages often are seen as a nuisance, many regard the value packs as something of a service.

☐ You can choose to have your coupon included in very specific, highly targeted mailings. You can also vary the frequency of the mailings. Because recipients don't expect discount coupons to be of high production quality, you can quickly alter the terms or message contained on your coupons, if you like, in subsequent mailings.

☐ For some reason, the small expiration date placed by some advertisers at the bottom of their discount coupon in the value pack is regarded with more urgency by recipients than a similar message would be through a traditional direct mail package. In other words, if your value pack coupon works, you will find out quickly.

☐ Value pack producers often are represented by traveling sales representatives who are eager for a sale and may be subject to negotiation.

Even among elite professional service providers such as doctors, dentists, lawyers, and so forth, the stigma of using value packs has long since subsided (see Figure 9-4). In any event, experimenting with the value pack is a low-cost, low-risk venture and one that can prove highly profitable for the shoestring marketer.

SEEING THE WRITING ON THE WALL

If you offer a business or professional service, chances are you work in a large office building with a directory posted in the lobby (see Figure 9-5). Depending on the nature of your business or profession, you may wish to consider expanding your listing in this directory.

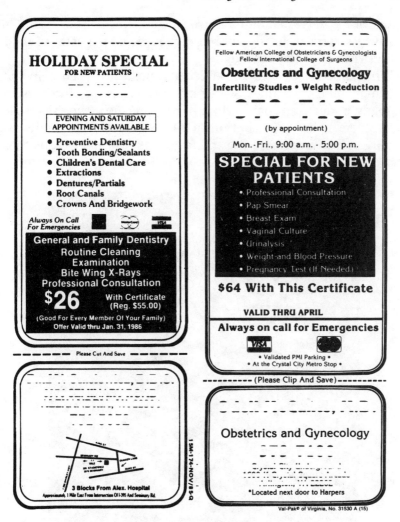

Figure 9-4. Many professionals, as well as other businesses, now use "value pack" coupons to promote their services. Reprinted with permission.

Millions of entrepreneurs across the country don't know how to gain desirable exposure through their building directories.

If you are an export consultant, then by all means have the name of your firm listed in alphabetical order followed by *export consultants*. Then in the "E" section of the directory, place another listing for *export consultants* followed by the name of your firm. This two-way system of listing your company assures greater visibility among visitors to the building.

In addition, if they can be added at little or no expense, include your name and the names of partners, principals, or officers of the company under your main listing in the directory. The extra space that you create between your office number and the one under you visually aids visitors who are trying to find you, as well as those who may be randomly exposed to your listing.

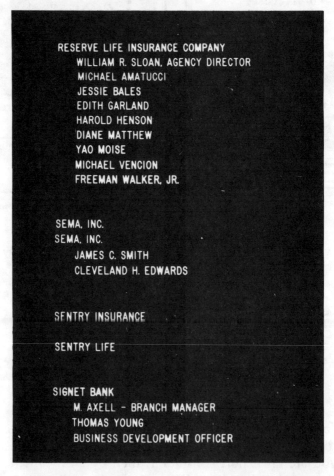

Figure 9-5. Give careful thought to the way your business is listed in the lobby directory.

In addition to using the building directory to increase your visibility, you also can use it and others in a surrounding two-block area for a limited, highly targeted marketing campaign. Barbers, dentists, manicurists, and numerous other professional and health service providers have used these building directories to produce instant mailing lists—everybody in the building is obviously at the same address.

Executive Services

One very effective, low-cost technique for attracting business from tenants of nearby office buildings is to design and post flyers offering special *executive services*. For example, the dry cleaner distributes handbills, flyers, or action letters to neighboring businesses, offering same day pick-up and delivery of suits. Or a dentist promises 35-minute turnaround time for routine examinations, check-ups, and teeth cleaning.

Actual Bulletin Boards

In every community there are libraries, universities, community colleges, high schools, and other institutions and businesses that provide bulletin board space for commercial advertisers. Depending on the product or service that you provide, the size of your business, and your desired target market, these free bulletin boards could be significant in support of your overall marketing campaign.

Those who provide typing and word processing services are able to readily attract new customers by posting messages in libraries and on school bulletin boards, particularly in university student unions and student activity halls. Bible sellers, correspondence schools, insurance companies, and encyclopedia manufacturers have known for years that the free literature display racks in the entranceway of supermarkets generate a continuous, inexpensive source of leads.

Take a walk around your community one day past the town hall, through condominium complexes, and into churches and meeting houses and you will quickly see a number of free or low-cost bulletin boards and other places for your printed literature.

Apartment villages and high-rise condominium complexes offer a unique bonanza for shoestring marketers who know how to take advantage of the potential opportunities that await. Many of these multiresidential developments have tables and ledges in the mail room, phone room or throughout, where, if literature distribution is not encouraged, it certainly is not disallowed. One notice on a condominium lobby bulletin board might be read by as many as 2000 people in the course of a few days.

In addition, with the advent of high speed copiers, desktop publishing, and inexpensive offset copying, many residential communities now produce their own flyers and newsletters. Some of these are very sophisticated. Advertising your products or services in these vehicles may be free in some cases, if they are looking for filler space; otherwise, the fee will be modest compared to other vehicles when you consider the number of people you will reach (see Figure 9-6).

The beauty of advertising in a residential complex publication is that you generally can obtain comprehensive information regarding the readers of such publications. For example, you know what the average unit sells for, what average rents are, how many people reside in the average unit, if they walk or drive to do their shopping, and so forth. I have known and observed entrepreneurs in Marina Del Rey, Dallas, Chicago, Atlanta, and Boston who have used these strategic bulletin boards to greatly enhance the client base and profitability of their businesses.

The magic of displaying your message in these forums is that most people read their condominium or apartment village newsletters with enthusiasm and interest that normally does not accrue to the voluminous pile of printed matter that they otherwise encounter through the Sunday paper, regional magazines, catalogs, and direct mail. In metropolitan areas, your display ad also provides you with a strategic advantage over those other businesses that fail to use this medium. In our nation's largest metro areas, the Yellow Pages are simply unwieldly. You couldn't find a business or service located three blocks away in under five minutes of intensive searching, because the phone books have grown so large and the listings so numerous that the convenient neighborhood product or service supplier is sunk in a sea of others.

The

House Special

Skyline
House

VOLUME VII   SEPTEMBER 1987   No. 8

FOX REALTY-ERA

For the BEST in Rental
Property Management

JoAnn Sisel
Property Manager

Sales & Rental

(2 blks. east of George Mason Dr.)

MLS   **ERA REAL ESTATE**

HERE'S A GREAT

IDEA!

FOR YOUR

CARPETS

Because it doesn't take long for hidden soil to become visible, and soon serious wear to take place. After that, it's downhill all the way. Let ServiceMaster remove soil to restore that deep-down fresh and colorful look that made you select your carpets in the first place.

ServiceMASTER   *the cleaning people who care®*

Figure 9-6. A local newsletter can be a good place to advertise your business.

Newsletter Editors Are Starving for Material

Throughout this book, I have refrained from recommending full-blown print advertisements in major publications. However, your message in professional, social, and civic newsletters can reach a highly targeted market for relatively little money (see Figure 9-7).

Figure 9-7. Typical ads in highly targeted newsletters and magazines. Note the appropriateness of each ad for the target audience.

150

Figure 9-7. (continued)

151

The NAD Broadcaster

Volume 9, Number 5   The National Association of the Deaf, 814 Thayer Avenue, Silver Spring, Maryland 20910   May, 1987

Figure 9-7. (continued)

Computer Digest

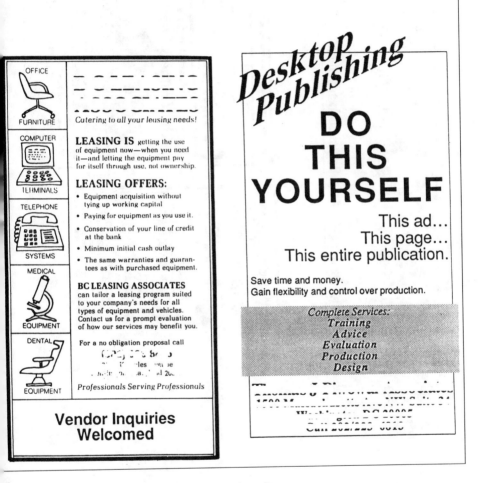

Figure 9-7. (continued)

Ride On!

Vol. XVI. No. 8   **Newsletter of the Washington Area Bicyclist Association**   August 1987

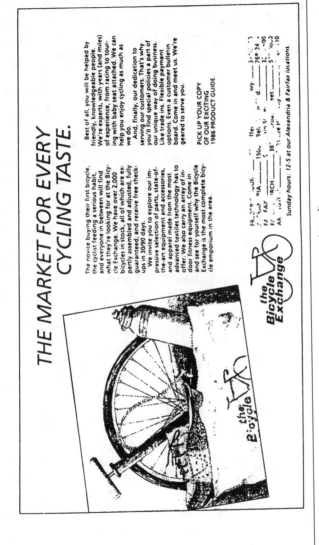

THE MARKET FOR EVERY CYCLING TASTE.

The novice buying their first bicycle, the cyclist feeding a serious habit, and everyone in between will find what they're looking for at the Bicycle Exchange. We have over 2,000 bicycles in stock, all of which are expertly assembled and adjusted, fully guaranteed, and receive free checkups in 30/90 days.

We invite you to explore our impressive selection of parts, state-of-the-art equipment and accessories, and apparel made from the most advanced textiles technology has to offer. We also carry an array of indoor fitness equipment. Come in and see for yourself why the Bicycle Exchange is the most complete bicycle emporium in the area.

Best of all, you will be helped by friendly, knowledgeable people. We're experts, with years (and miles) of experience, from racing to touring with baby seat attached. We can help you enjoy cycling as much as we do.

And, finally, our dedication to serving our customers. That's why you'll find special policies a part of our unique way of doing business. Like trade ins. Flexible payment options. Even a customer bulletin board. Come in and meet us. We're geared to serve you.

PICK UP YOUR COPY
OF OUR EXCITING
1986 PRODUCT GUIDE.

the Bicycle Exchange

Sunday hours: 12-5 at our Alexandria & Fairfax locations.

Figure 9-7. (continued)

155

With the continued demassification of society, as described by Alvin Tofler in *Future Shock* (New York: William Morrow, 1969), the effectiveness of advertising in the smaller, highly targeted vehicles will increase. Also consider college newspapers and suburban shoppers' guides; however, in many instances the price of advertising in these publications is not the bargain of the aforementioned publications, and competition once again becomes keen.

Suburban shoppers' guides, for example, may contain 100 or more advertisements and may be distributed to 50,000 or more residents of the community. Thus, it becomes as easy for your ad to get lost in these publications as it would be in the Sunday edition of *The Denver Post* or *The Des Moines Register*.

When you examine the various community bulletin boards in your area, also check for small publications, newsletters, and flyers. Write to or telephone specific professional groups in your area to obtain sample copies of their publications. Also ask condominium and residential community managers for their publications. The key to getting a free copy simply is to mention that you are interested in exploring the possibilities of advertising.

10

THE LUNCH
AND
DINNER CIRCUIT

Singleness of purpose is one of the chief essentials for success in life, no matter what may be one's aim.

John D. Rockefeller, Jr.

The potential of marketing via professional luncheons and dinners first hit me while I was attending a luncheon at the Greater Washington Society of Association Executives. As a speaker and author, I had joined this prestigious group of 1800 association executives and suppliers in order to become better known and to be retained as a speaker for local associations. GWSAE's monthly luncheon program was open to all members of the association, including association directors, deputy directors, and the various department heads one might find within an association, such as Manager of Membership Services, Education, New Member Development, and so on.

About one third of the members of the association were suppliers. These were people like myself who had a service they wished to offer and entrepreneurs who promoted an actual product, such as computer equipment, labeling devices, and office supplies. The concept of joining professional groups composed of your targets, attending luncheons, and making contacts probably is not new to you. However, the low-budget, highly effective marketing strategy I am about to describe to you is a new concept.

GWSAE's luncheons were held in the large banquet halls of local hotels. Ten people were seated at each circular table with a total audience of between 120 and 200 people. Once a month, for a modest fee, I was able to interact with nine other people at my table and on a yearly basis more than 100. Now, consider for a moment the possibility of calling on 108 new prospects in 24 hours. (See table below.) Even if you add a half hour of preparation time before the luncheon and a half hour afterwards for a total of 36 hours invested per year, you are still able to average three new prospects per hour of time invested.

9 people seated per table	× 12 luncheons per year	=	108 contacts
12 luncheons per year	× 2 hours per luncheon	=	24 hours

Like most associations, the Greater Washington Society of Association Executives publishes a high quality membership directory on an annual basis. At each roundtable, eight or nine of the other people seated were listed in the directory. Even if someone at the table was not listed in the directory, the large prominent name badges, worn by all, quickly revealed names, positions, and locations.

One afternoon it hit me. What a fabulous method of prospecting this was! When I got home, I quickly refined my technique. At the next monthly luncheon I came prepared. I carried a GWSAE directory, 15 stamped envelopes, and 15 self-addressed stamped envelopes, 15 pages of my stationery, 15 of my article reprints, and 25 business cards in my briefcase. Like any good product or service vendor, I made as many contacts as I could in the lobby before everyone was allowed into the banquet hall. During this time, I routinely exchanged four or five business cards. Once inside the luncheon room, unless I met someone with whom I had a particularly strong connection, I headed for a table on the far side or one at which I had not yet met anyone. Thus I positioned myself to meet nine more people.

SUBTLE AND SAVVY

Often, following the brief benediction, someone at the table would suggest we all introduce ourselves. In those cases, my task was doubly aided. During the introductions, I took notes in my lap of what they had said, knowing that this would be the start of marketing intelligence I would use later in communicating with them.

When it was my turn, I always paused for a second to make sure I had the attention of everyone at the table. Then, in a much slower and slightly louder voice than everyone else's, I clearly told them my name, what I did, and then made a humorous statement such as, "I help association meeting planners look good."

As the luncheon went on, I learned to position the membership directory within my briefcase so that I could sneak peeks without anyone else knowing exactly what I was looking at. These peeks provided me with instant and very usable information. For example, if Mary Smith was from the XYZ Association in Reston, Virginia, I would use whatever information was listed about her and her association immediately in conversation with her. "Oh, you are located out in Reston. That is a wonderful area for. . . ."

During the course of the lunch, as difficult as it may seem, I always was able to speak with each person at the table, if only for a few moments. This personal contact during the lunch proved to be very valuable. Immediately following the lunch, it was customary for most people to bolt for the door. I bid farewell to as many people at the table as possible with an open-ended message, such as "Let's keep in touch" or "See you at the next luncheon." Or, if our personal conversation had really gotten rolling, I'd say, "I will be sure to send you that information I mentioned."

Now the *piece de resistance.* Before leaving the hotel area, I neatly hand-addressed envelopes to those I had met at my table and anyone else I had met in the lobby or had seen again after meeting at a previous luncheon meeting. I then enclosed brief personalized notes to them, either based on what we had discussed or of a general nature, such as "Nice meeting you at the GWSAE luncheon last Thursday. I would like to give you a call regarding. . . ." I also enclosed with the letter an article reprint and my business card.

If I had not already obtained their business card, I included a self-addressed stamped envelope and asked them to send their card to me.

This system was marvelous. In a short time I was able to build up my Rolodex. I had a number of association and supplier contacts around town who were much more easily sold when I called upon them in person at their place of business, or when I saw them again at another association meeting. Because I was able to send out the letters so quickly—that very same day—the impact of their meeting me and getting a letter the next day helped establish me as a known player in their environment.

GROUPS, GROUPS, GROUPS

Independent of whether you sell a product or service locally, regionally, or nationally, there is a variety of civic, trade, industrial, and professional groups in which you can make strong prospecting contacts. Many groups today, such as the Society of Association Executives, or purchasing councils, have created a category called *associate member*. The associate member might not actively work in the business or profession for whom the group was formed. However, in order to increase revenues and as a service to their members, many associations recognize the value of allowing associate members—essentially suppliers to full members—into the group (see table on next page).

Two directories provide the names and addresses of thousands of professional and trade associations throughout the United States. These directories, found in the reference section of *any* library, are the *National Trade and Professional Association* directory (NTPA), and *Gale's Encyclopedia of Associations*. Another is the *Directory of Conventions*, published by Successful Meetings Incorporated. The *Directory of Conventions* provides the names, addresses, and phone numbers of specific groups that have scheduled conventions up to two years in advance. The directory is arranged geographically and even lists the number of attendees.

Locally, you can tap into the vast professional luncheon circuit by referring to the business calendar section of your local newspaper. Routinely, this calendar provides the names of the

Associate Members Who Could Market Effectively to Associations

Full Membership Category	Associate Members Who Could Effectively Market
Aerospace manufacturers	Subcontractors of selected parts
Association executives	Speakers, trainers, workshop leaders
Association executives	Personnel agencies, temporary service agencies
Home builders	Roofers, electrical contractors, masons
Small business entrepreneurs	Consultants, accountants, insurance agents
Retail merchants	Security services, janitorial services
Purchasing agents	Product and service vendors
Dental societies	Dental suppliers, advertising agents
Architects	Builders and developers
Realtors	Insurance agents, brokers
Plumbers	Pipe supply distributors
Club managers	Linen suppliers, swimming pool supply companies
Landscapers	Garden suppliers, hardware vendors
Speakers	Cassette duplicators, speaking coaches
Singers	Voice teachers
Musicians	Musical suppliers
Theater directors, actors	Theatrical suppliers

groups that are meeting, where they will be meeting, either the names or telephone numbers of the meeting planners, the cost of the luncheon, and the topic for the speaker that day.

If you want to follow my strategy and become a member of your area Society of Association Executives, contact the American Society of Association Executives at 1575 I Street, NW, Washington, DC 20005, (202)626-ASAE, and ask for the name of the nearest association executive group in your area.

Another simple procedure for targeting key groups is to ask your best clients or customers which groups they belong to. This will give you an immediate list of at least three and probably as many as 12 local groups. Obviously your time and resources are limited, so you want to choose the group with the most lucrative targets.

By asking your key customers and clients which groups they belong to, you are reasonably assured of encountering clones of your clients and customers. Why? Like meets with like. Your best customers retain membership in those associations that offer the greatest value or for which there is some key strategic or competitive advantage. Similarly, the prospects you wish to target in many ways operate or at least think like your best customers.

BECOMING ONE OF US

As I pointed out in *Marketing Your Consulting and Professional Services* (New York: John Wiley & Sons, 1985), the reason most entrepreneurs are not successful on the rubber chicken or dinner circuit is that they give up too soon and assume that no one is really interested in them. They are, as my friend Griff Doyle says, the "short hitters." The key to making the circuit work for you is to take the initiative. Be professionally aggressive and attend often enough that you are perceived as an insider.

Once you become one of the gang, your marketing task becomes that much easier. The key to effectively working the circuit is to attend the meetings of the few key groups you have targeted. Since you can't be everywhere at once, have your sales manager, spouse, field rep, or other company representatives join you in this function.

In all cases, the number of prospects you can meet, if you and your representatives properly "work" the lunch or dinner circuit, far exceeds the number you could meet by traveling around town honoring appointments. Granted, as a follow-up you probably will travel around town to meet with the contacts you have made. The key difference is you will be encountering them for the second time and you will be entering any new business discussion at an entirely different level—one of associate, peer, or perhaps even friend. This raises the value and effectiveness of these sales calls and greatly reduces overall marketing expense.

Over the years, I have observed others who have used the luncheon and dinner circuit to forge links with particular groups that were so strong that, eventually, doing business with them became second nature to the group.

One cassette duplication manufacturer, for example, joined a local group of professional speakers, served on their board for several years, and even became president for a year. Through his association with the speakers' group, the cassette entrepreneur became so well known to speakers in his community that for years thereafter all new members of the group were immediately referred to him by senior members when they needed cassette duplication services. He had, in essence, created a system of new leads and referrals without end.

In time, he found that only random appearances were necessary to maintain his strong connection with the association. And, as the need to attend each meeting diminished, he initiated other associations in serial fashion.

You Were Not That Hungry Anyway, Were You?

Make no mistake: Working the luncheon and dinner circuit is hard work. But it is relatively inexpensive in terms of cash outlay, it pays off in the long run, and, if handled properly, it pays off in the short run, too. As with most budget marketing techniques, time rather than a large cash investment is all that is required. If you are able to plan your appointments so that you are already in the vicinity, this marketing strategy need not be disruptive.

Practically speaking, if you are handling your marketing task effectively, you won't be digesting your lunch or dinner well (hence the name rubber chicken). Those who represent you at meetings that you cannot attend should be advised of this fact. The luncheon or dinner is simply a ticket to interact with those who have come to assemble. It never was intended for nourishment.

Here are a few key do's and don'ts to remember.

Do:

☐ Review the group's newsletter or publication in advance for timely topics, key names, and discussion points.

☐ Arrive early, make a stop in the restroom, and be ready for action.

☐ Try to take a seat facing the speaker.

☐ Always say your name slowly, loudly, and clearly.

☐ Show interest in what the other people have to say.

☐ Quickly get to know the president and officers of the association

☐ Ask for the business cards of others. This in turn, prompts them to ask for your business card.

☐ Send out your follow-up letters immediately following the event. Don't wait until you get home or arrive at the next stop, no matter how tired you are.

Don't:

☐ Arrive late, or with your briefcase unprepared.

☐ Come on too strong or be pushy.

☐ Order chicken or any other selection that involves maneuvering around a bone.

☐ Expect to eat a full meal, make conversation with everyone at the table, take follow-up notes, and avoid indigestion.

☐ Smoke.

☐ Be disruptive during the formal presentation.

☐ Discount the value of anyone you meet at these groups toward your overall marketing effort.

☐ Get into a conversation with one or two people at the table to the exclusion of all the rest.

☐ Cut and run as soon as the meeting is over.

To See and Be Seen

A by-product of working the circuit is your ability to see old contacts regularly, meet new contacts, and gather information that will help your overall marketing program. Even if a particular luncheon offers no true prospects, the insider information and tips that you learn during the formal presentation and in conversation with others around the table will still be worth the price of admission. Nothing is worse than armchair analysis—trying to determine the needs and wants of your target market from your desk. The luncheon circuit can be used quite effectively as a means of learning how to modify or improve your marketing approach. Where else will people readily tell you about their business problems, successes, and current "Matterhorns"?

Consider also that when you and your representatives make contact with professionals in targeted groups, you are making contact with people at the top. Generally speaking, junior associates are not assigned responsibility for the luncheon circuit. Why? Entrepreneurs of successful businesses recognize the need to make high level contact themselves. The rainmaker of any firm with less than 15 people usually is the president him/herself.

For larger companies, even if you don't meet the association director, president, or top executive, those you meet will have significant responsibility and decision-making authority. This personal contact often enables you to cut through the organizational maze and go right to the top.

The Players and the Scorecards

One way to facilitate your marketing effectiveness on the lunch and dinner circuit is to obtain in advance the directories or membership rosters of the groups you have targeted. On a local basis, many groups publish a membership roster that is available free to other members or for a nominal charge. Many groups also make their roster available to nonmembers, usually for a $10 or $20 charge. Obviously, some groups keep their membership lists private and thus, to obtain one, you will have to leverage your relationship with an existing member of the targeted group.

Particularly for groups who publish a newsletter or some type of monthly publication, a membership roster or subscription list exists and sometimes is available for a fee. Some groups offer their list of labels for one-time use as an added means of generating revenue. In other cases you may be able to obtain the membership roster as barter for some service that you provide (see Chapter 11).

Local groups affiliated with national organizations may not have their own membership rosters. However, their members may be listed in the national roster. There are several ways to obtain such membership rosters and directories.

First, consult *The Directory of Directories*. This Gale Press publication is found in virtually every library's reference section and contains the names of thousands of directories cross-indexed by name, subject, and location. *The Directory of Directories* is a gold mine for the entrepreneur who wants to market on a shoestring and be very effective. Another alternative is the *National Trade and Professional Association* directory, which notes whether or not a particular association publishes a membership roster.

Finally, you can always write to the membership director of a national association and request information about publications in this area.

Fortunately, you will find in most instances that the membership directories are available, albeit for a stiff fee of $50 or more. When you consider the value of obtaining names in this way, however, and particularly scouting in advance those whom you wish to meet on the luncheon circuit, this is a masterstroke of low-cost marketing effectiveness. Often your local library will have copies of association membership rosters. By phoning the reference desk you may obtain information needed to determine what your local library is holding.

Particularly in the case of suppliers and tradespeople, your library may well contain a copy of the local Blue Book. These are membership directories published and distributed by the local association as a marketing vehicle for the association's own members. Your goal is to obtain these directories and use a reverse procedure.

A strategy of obtaining membership lists and rosters works best in combination with actually meeting the members face to face. Hence, the lunch and dinner circuit, combined with a little research and a little preparation, is for many shoestring marketers the most effective ploy.

11

THE UNDERGROUND ECONOMY: BARTERING AND SWAPPING

We are all of us richer than we think we are.

Michel de Montaigne

We all have some background in bartering starting with our early exchanges of baseball cards and our agreements to mow the lawn or babysit for kids in return for use of the family car. Business bartering ranges from brief local exchanges, often called *trade-outs* (i.e., "If you'll put my poster in your restaurant window, I'll print your 'Today's Special' menu insert at my copy shop for free.") to complex international *countertrade* involving corporate inventory exchanges arranged by large firms that act as middlemen in multinational barter.

For businesses with tight marketing budgets, barter can be a valuable alternative to paying cash for advertising, printing materials, client and customer leads, media exposure, and advice. Instead of writing a check, you pay with your own services (usually entailing an expenditure of time rather than money, but often consuming only what might have been "down time", anyway) or goods (which reflect only the wholesale cost to you and which may represent inventory that would have been difficult to move otherwise).

167

I'LL SCRATCH YOUR BACK IF . . .

The U.S. Department of Commerce estimates the value of barter transactions at well over $20 million per year, and some analysts put the number of U.S. companies engaged in barter at over 10,000. While many of the companies that have used barter are giants like General Electric, National Semiconductor Corporation, and Citicorp, hundreds of small companies engage in it as a way of obtaining services that simply would not be affordable otherwise.

For example, when two struggling entrepreneurs opened the Purple House women's clothing store in a small Western town, they soon had little cash left for advertising. Nevertheless, they were able to barter for several full-page, back cover ads in the local theater's playbill by providing clothing from their inventory for use in theater productions. Since they bargained to exchange only end-of-season items that were due for drastic price reductions, the advertisements cost them less than half of what would have been the cash outlay.

Similarly, early in my career as a marketing consultant, I provided consultation services to an office support company that specialized in copying, typing, word processing, etc. In exchange for my services, I was permitted unlimited access to their copier for printing my own promotional materials. Later, when I assisted an advertising professional in structuring his book, he gave me a design for a high quality, four-color brochure. This hour-for-hour exchange allowed us both to obtain valuable assistance without opening our checkbooks.

Successful bartering may include exchanges of goods for goods, services for services, or goods for services. In negotiating, however, you particularly need to concern yourself with value for value. You'll need to estimate the dollar value of the goods or services you are willing to exchange and compare that to the dollar value of whatever you will receive in return. When you make these comparisons, be careful not to confuse apples with oranges by comparing wholesale costs or discounted prices with retail prices or full costs.

If you are exchanging ten hours of time on your company computer for printing 5000 copies of your brochure, figure out the real cash outlay that would have to be paid for each if no barter were involved. If your computer time is more valuable than the printing, you may need to limit the number of hours or increase the number of brochures you want.

The key to successful bartering is to be innovative, creative, *and* realistic. Think of anything and everything you might have to offer in exchange for goods and services that can help your marketing effort, but don't get so carried away with the idea that you cheat yourself. While bartering is never quite cost-free, it is an excellent opportunity to obtain marketing assistance without an actual cash outlay. If you can answer the following questions affirmatively, the chances are good that your business could benefit from using barter as a low-cost way to market your products or services.

- ☐ Do you have inventory or services that would sometimes seem a less costly form of payment than cash?
- ☐ Are there marketing strategies you would like to use but don't use because you feel you cannot afford to pay for them?
- ☐ Could you use some marketing advice, but find yourself reluctant to pay for it because you're not sure how valuable it will be?
- ☐ Are you willing to think creatively about what you can give and get without an exchange of money?

Michael Gershman regularly writes about marketing and also acts as a consultant to several corporations. Recently he published *Smarter Barter: A Guide for Corporations, Professionals and Small Businesses* (New York: Viking Press, 1986), suggesting that readers examine their own priorities in order to determine exactly how and what to barter. "For example," writes Gershmann, "let's say your number one priority is to promote old merchandise in order to dispose of it (to make way for a new line). Then, bartering for media might offer a likely solution to your problem."

If you seek new buyers for your goods and services, working through a trade exchange or a corporate barter broker might make the most sense. Many businesses turn to barter companies to conduct the complex, often multinational trades that are necessary when inventory isn't moving satisfactorily. These companies find outlets for products and pay for them in trade.

For example, Mediators, Inc., a marketing and media buying firm, trades advertising space in exchange for goods at wholesale price and then finds another source or sources, perhaps overseas, willing to pay for them. Richard Manney, founder and chief executive officer of Mediators, notes, "Unlike cash, every organization has *alternative capital* available. Alternative capital is the value of an organization's products, services, and manufacturing capacity."

Barter Beware

While there is ample opportunity for barter arrangements that work in everybody's favor, there are also ample examples of barter turned sour. Typically, this happens when the exchange negotiated is not actually value for value or when too little thought went into the arrangement from the beginning.

Michael Gershman offers the following Ten Commandments of Barter to help assure smooth, equitable barter arrangements:

1. Know why you're trading. This seems elementary, but trading has a way of igniting elementary passions and causing even the most rational business people to get caught up in the excitement of the process. If your primary objective is conserving cash, stick to it. If you want to make sure that products are sold through noncompetitive outlets, stick to it. If you're looking for media, don't get sidetracked with hotel facilities you may not be able to retrade.

2. Investigate many alternatives. Don't put all your eggs into one basket. Working on a single opportunity makes you more vulnerable to accepting a low offer because it's the only offer. If you feel trade exchanges are your best bet, talk to three or four of them. If you're unsure about which approach to use, interview several different kinds of companies. Many bartering mistakes can be avoided with some elementary patience. If you give bartering as much thought and care as the other parts of your business, you'll learn quickly how to spot what is truly the best alternative for you.

3. Keep a tight rein on your ego. Marketing light blue catcher's mitts was a fine idea at the time, but that time is past. You made a

mistake. Face it, and you may be able to salvage something. Who knows? Maybe it's a hot color in Venezuela.

4. Swap what is truly swappable at the right time and place. Don't try to trade skis in May or rollerskates in Samoa. Research alternative distribution outlets for your product thoroughly, and then decide on a timing and placement strategy to dispose of your inventory.

5. Maintain realistic goals. Going into the barter marketplace requires the tacit admission that you can't get the cash price you want for your products or services—that's the reason you're bartering. It stands to reason, then, that you should have realistic expectations of what you can get in exchange.

6. Don't try to trade over the telephone. There's a certain amount of chemistry to a trade that doesn't transmit well over the phone lines. While talking on the telephone, people can be distracted by office happenings and may turn down what might be as good a swap for them as for you. Set up a meeting in person, prepare what you're going to say, be persuasive, listen as well as you speak to your trading partners' needs, and you'll make a trade.

7. Don't take rejection personally. Because trading can be an intense and personal experience, novice barterers often become discouraged when their offers are rejected. Make another offer. If your prospective trading partner wasn't interested, he or she wouldn't be listening to you in the first place. Sometimes you can make exactly the same offer but present it a bit differently and wind up making a deal.

8. Use your imagination. If a simple reciprocal swap won't work, try thinking up an alternative that might become a three-way deal. For instance, if you've decided to trade scrap steel and are offered rental car vouchers when you really want magazine advertising, it may pay off to take the vouchers in hopes of retrading them later for the print ads you really want. A valuable trading commodity like rental car credits can be "banked" and retraded relatively quickly.

9. Get an outside appraisal of your commodity's worth. A potential trading partner will put greater credence in the Kelly Blue Book price for your 1979 Ford Fairlane than your own wild guess.

Ask your trading partner for similar information, if possible, in order to provide a starting point for negotiations.

10. Put your deal into contract form. In the afterglow of a successful trade, particularly at the beginning of your bartering career, you may be inclined to take someone's word on a given element of the deal. Resist that impulse. Make the contract as specific as possible. If you agree to trade 5000 widgets for $5000 worth of radio time, make sure you specify the dates and the time of day that the commercials must run in order to fulfill the contract.

In addition to these commandments, keep in mind that negotiating for barter is not an adversary situation. You are looking for a result whereby everybody wins and everybody saves money.

International Countertrade

The U.S. Department of Commerce is an excellent source of information on barter, especially on more complex international countertrade practices. If your goal is to establish marketing presence overseas, then you could employ a trading company or work through a countertrade specialist. The Commerce Department publication *International Countertrade: A Guide for Managers and Executives* is a 90-page guide that defines and describes types of countertrade, U.S. and foreign regulations affecting them, and government support services available. (To order, write to the U.S. Government Printing Office, Washington, DC 20402. Stock number: 003-009-00-435-7)

Advertisements for Services

Have you ever wondered why you frequently see advertisements for printing companies on the back of a flyer, in a playbill, or even in a schedule of events for a state fair? It is usually because the printing company provided typesetting, layout, and/or printing services for the material in which the advertisement appears. Instead of receiving payment in cash, however, they have arranged a barter exchange for advertising space.

This type of exchange is valuable for everybody involved. The people who need the printed material may have space available that wouldn't have been purchased by another company, anyway, so the cost of reserving that space for the printing company is negotiable. The printing company generally can negotiate to get the ad space at a much lower cost than they would have paid in cash. That is, if they provide layout services for which they would usually charge $500, and the firm needing the printed material is eager to avoid a cash outlay, the barter may result in ad space for which well over $500 would have been charged to advertisers paying in cash. Other publications you might try include:

□ Flight publications

□ Art magazines

□ Automotive and motorcycle publications

□ Business opportunity magazines

□ Children's magazine

□ Sporting club publications

□ Science magazines

□ University or alumni publications

□ Weekly newspapers

□ Women's magazines

□ Confession magazines

□ Consumer services magazines

□ Weekly newspapers

□ Detective magazines

□ Financial newsletters

□ Food magazines

□ Association publications

□ Health magazines

□ Home and garden magazines

□ Hard rock magazines

□ Pet owners publications

□ Nature and ecology publications

□ Publications directed towards minority groups

□ Educators newsletters

□ Regional publications

□ Spiritual publications

□ Hobby and craft publications
□ Senior citizens' magazines
□ Trade and professional journals
□ Camping publications
□ Union publications
□ Yellow Pages or phone books

Barter in exchange for advertising can be done by numerous types of companies and is especially relevant for those that are service oriented. For example:

□ A local polling/survey firm might exchange a survey of radio listening habits for radio advertisements on an interested station.

□ An architectural firm may design a new office layout for a magazine willing to give them advertising space in several issues.

□ A company specializing in proposal writing for clients may write a proposal for state funding for a radio station wishing to do a public interest series on how to conserve water. In turn, the proposal writing firm may receive advertising time on that radio station.

□ A public relations firm may advise a weekly newspaper on strategies for increasing its readership in exchange for advertising space in the newspaper.

□ A photographic studio may take photos that a graphic artist wants to use in a brochure in exchange for layout services for the photo studio magazine ads.

When considering how your company might be able to barter for advertising space, it is helpful to think in terms of *who* is involved in the design and placement of advertisements and *what* you can do for those entities. For example, what services (or goods) can you provide to these businesses?

□ Publishers
□ Printers
□ Photographers

□ Graphic artists
□ Radio and television stations
□ Newspaper and magazines
□ Sign and billboard companies

Each of the businesses or professions listed above can be key in the development and placement of your advertisements, and all would require a significant cash outlay if you could not barter for their services.

In addition, be sure to think of smaller publication outlets for your advertising that may be more receptive to barter than your large daily newspaper or monthly city magazine. Shoppers guides, want ad publications, and programs for a variety of events represent targets of opportunity for bartered advertising.

In bartering for advertising, it is important to think of advertising in its broadest sense—that is, any outlet for increased exposure for your business. When I began publishing articles in magazines and journals, some paid very little. However, I was able to negotiate for extended author's biographies with my articles; these carried enough information to advertise my services and my books. From feedback I received, it became apparent that those biographies provided advertising exposure equal to or beyond the value of my time spent writing the articles.

In another barter arrangement to receive greater exposure for my business, I was able to negotiate for the services of Joe Shafran, a media placement consultant in Washington, DC, and president of *You're on the Air!* Joe wanted to open some new markets. I provided him with research and consulting services, and ultimately developed the strategies he needed. In turn, he was able to place me on four television and eight radio talk shows in New York, Boston, Hartford, and Washington, DC. The cash outlay for this media brokerage service would have been considerable; instead, I was able to pay with my time.

Referral Swaps

It is often said that the best way to get new clients is by word of mouth. A satisfied client or customer tells a friend about your business. This immediately establishes a higher level of trust than when someone sees your media advertisements or reads your printed literature. Another type of word-of-mouth recommendation happens when a satisfied client of one business is referred to you by that business. Obviously, this works in the case of businesses that are not in competition, and it is very valuable in the case of service-oriented businesses. Such would be the case when a lawyer refers one of her clients to an accountant.

When two service businesses are complementary, this type of referral swap can work exceedingly well. Some examples of businesses that can benefit from referring one another include:

□ Architects and realtors

□ Architects and interior designers

□ Veterinarians and pet shop owners

□ Computer systems consultants and management consultants

□ Financial systems consultants and management consultants

□ Public relations consultants and printers

□ Insurance agents and stock brokers

□ Personal financial consultants and insurance agents

□ Computer programmers and computer sales agents

□ Moving companies and realtors

□ Management trainers and organizational consultants

□ Editors/proofreaders and typesetters/printers

□ Carpenters and hardware supply agents

□ Stockbrokers and accountants

The list could go on and on, and it takes only a bit of imagination to determine who is in a field that has new clients or customers you might want to approach as prospects for your own business.

Referral swapping generally works best in face-to-face meetings among professionals with whom you already have had some contact. For example, if you operate an advertising agency, you probably are in regular contact with one or more businesses that print flyers, posters, and business cards for you and your clients. Those same printing firms get a lot of walk-in customers who bring items to be printed. These customers may not have used an advertising agency to develop new concepts and media plans. However, they might need an advertising agency more than they realize—preferably yours.

At the same time, many of your clients may need the services of a reliable printer they can use for reports and booklets that do not necessarily go through your advertising agency. At a meeting with the head of your printing firm, you can discuss the idea of a referral swap and iron out details of types and numbers of likely clients to refer to one another.

You can arrange a periodic formal swap of five or more really good prospects, or you can establish an ongoing method by which you simply phone one another whenever someone known to one seems a likely client for the other. If the potential clients are likely to result in real sales or contracts, it also can be useful for two businesses engaged in referral swaps to make calls for one another. In other words, an accountant paves the way for an insurance agent by calling five of his/her best clients and mentioning the insurance company. The insurance agent calls five of his/her clients to introduce the accountant. Both later follow with calls of their own.

Referral swaps can be developed with creative twists that provide a slight variation on the clients for clients trade. For example, moving companies work with realtors who know when houses are being sold and can refer potential clients who are going to need movers. In exchange for this, the moving company offers a discount to clients of the real estate firm. Thus, the real estate company can advertise "20% discount to our clients on moving and storage, from Speedy Moving and Storage." This helps the real estate firm get clients by offering a benefit that other firms may not have, and it helps the moving firm get clients by directly contacting people who are selling their homes.

Rolodex Reviews

The Rolodex review takes the concept of referral swapping one step further. In this mode, two noncompeting business owners go into one another's offices and look through name and address files to discover potential new clients and discuss how best to approach them. The idea is to uncover new clients, contacts, and leads.

For example, Terry Lynton and Marv Geste discovered over hamburgers at a neighborhood barbeque that they were both involved in starting new businesses with complementary client lists. Terry, a realtor who had started a business specializing in unimproved land, suggested an exploratory meeting with Marv, an architect who often worked with small-scale builders and developers. They quickly realized that Marv had many contacts among builders who always had an eye out for the next parcel of land to buy and develop and that Terry sold land to many individuals looking for an architect. They decided that their best method of exchanging potential new clients would be to explore one another's client files, seeking names and information about target contacts.

After the initial file search, each had come up with about six good prospects. They exchanged more information on these and discussed how to approach them from Terry's real estate angle and Marv's architectural angle. Their exchange proved so valuable that they repeat it quarterly, although they also refer to each other by word of mouth in between the formal review of files.

Like any swap, this exchange requires that two businesses feel they are getting equal value from their efforts. It will fail if one individual finds there are no valuable leads to be discovered in the other's files. But it can be an exceedingly beneficial way to test the waters and determine whether a seemingly complementary business can indeed provide leads. When using this method of client barter, communication is an essential ingredient. The exchange doesn't just stop with a glimpse into the files of another office. It requires ongoing discussions to uncover details about potential clients that may not be apparent on paper.

Tip Clubs

Tip clubs are formed expressly for the purpose of exchanging word-of-mouth marketing leads. Generally organized by geographic area (i.e., a group on the west side of Bakersfield, California or along the shore in Westport, Connecticut), these clubs may have as few as five members or as many as several dozen.

Typically they are comprised of professional service providers who do not compete, such as an insurance agent and a tax accountant. To keep all existing members happy, no rivals are allowed to join, so there will be only one tax accountant per club and so on. They work best when the individuals involved are of equal status rather than rookies mixed with veterans. Thus, the leads provided tend to have equal potential to all involved.

At a tip club meeting, a builder may alert the group to a new office building being planned and may offer the names of some companies already signed up to lease space. He will probably have contact names and phone numbers for key representatives at the various companies moving into the new offices. This is certainly an aid to the club member who is a consultant in office space design and the member who owns an office moving company. The advertising executive who is present may even want to approach some of the companies moving to the new building about ad campaigns based on "We're moving to serve you better."

That same advertising executive may have two new clients, developers who have recently moved to the area. Sharing those names can be particularly valuable to the builder in the group, and to some others. The strength of such groups is based on the interconnection of potential clients. By meeting with one another, members get advance notice of "who is doing what" in their area and increase their chances of being the first to approach a target client or company.

For example, the information exchanged in the above example certainly would be useful to anyone in the business of office janitorial services, carpet installation, or even providing greenery to offices. While not every name mentioned may be a potential client for all others, each member should come away from meetings with at least some valuable leads.

If there is no formal tip club in your area, you can start one with informal lunch meetings with just a few individuals involved in businesses complementary to yours. It will grow as discussions produce ideas for others who might avail themselves of similar client information.

Reciprocal Discount Arrangements

Have you ever seen an ad in the paper with a little blurb at the bottom of the page reading "Located next to Joe's Hardware." Sometimes the purpose of this is to give the customer a quick idea of where the business is located, capitalizing on the fact that everyone in town knows the location of Joe's Hardware.

More and more frequently, however, this arrangement is *designed* to refer to the business neighbor in one another's ads. Joe's Hardware benefits because many people in town go to its neighbor, Phil's Pizza. If half the town previously knew about each of the businesses, now most people are exposed to both of them. Meanwhile, each business has increased its customer base at virtually no extra expense.

Another category of reciprocal arrangements is a discount between two complementary product or service vendors. An example would be a stereo store offering discounts on records.

Restaurants lure hungry theatre patrons and moviegoers with: "After the show" or "Free bottle of wine with dinner before the play." This is a good example of reciprocal discounts. Many people will want to eat before or after seeing a play or movie, and the restaurant owners use this to their advantage. In the Washington, DC area, The American Cafe, a high class multilocation restaurant serving fancy and exotic dishes, provides a list of special services to people going to see a show at Wolf Trap Farm Park, an upper-level performance center located in the Virginia suburbs of Washington, DC. The American Cafe uses the standard "before or after the play" advertising, offers frequent round-trip buses to the park, and will even cater a fully prepared, albeit expensive, picnic meal to be provided at the tables near the park's entrance.

Bartering for Space

If you have anything to offer merchants in your area, you are in a good position to barter for space in their establishments for displaying your posters, stacking your brochures, or placing other types of advertising. In restaurants, for example, you might notice "table tents" that advertise upcoming events at a local museum or community theatre. Those who run the museum or theatre probably have exchanged free tickets to restaurant personnel for the table space or have allocated window space or bulletin board space in their establishments for restaurant advertising.

The cost of advertising space and of distributing marketing literature by mail or hand can become prohibitive if you have to pay for it in cash. So, anything you can do to barter for space will save you substantial marketing dollars.

One window cleaning firm has advertised effectively for years with posters in the windows of local storefront merchants: "Get your windows as clean as this." In exchange for this window space, the firm regularly cleans the windows in which it places its posters at no cost. Similarly, a restaurant in a large urban area approached a number of trendy clothing boutiques nearby about window space. Their posters, designed especially for these windows, proclaim, "Give that new dress the evening out it deserves." In exchange, the restaurant gives "two meals for the price of one" coupons to the management of the boutiques that display its posters.

It takes creativity to determine likely exchanges for advertising space, and you can start by thinking of the types of spaces your local merchants can offer, such as:

- □ Countertops for your brochures
- □ Bulletin boards for your flyers
- □ Windows for your posters
- □ Restaurant tables for your table tents
- □ Dressing room mirrors for your decals
- □ Floor space for your samples

Remember that this type of advertising is not a one-time effort. Flyers on windows will get worn and torn and need to be replaced with new ones. Table tents about events need to be updated, and brochures on countertops need to be replenished regularly. You cannot expect the merchant giving you space also to maintain that space for you or to graciously house torn posters or stained table tents.

When you do decide to barter for advertising space, it is important to decide before you approach a merchant exactly what you have to offer and what the space is worth to you.

12

SIXTEEN MORE LOW-COST MARKETING TIPS

Luck is not something you can mention in the presence of self-made men.

E.B. White

In this last chapter we will look at a potpourri of highly effective shoestring marketing techniques that have been profitable to entrepreneurs in a variety of businesses. These are not presented in any particular order; indeed, their importance will vary greatly depending on the nature of the product or service that you provide and the particulars of your business operation.

1. Obtaining Free Marketing Surveys and Advice

Throughout the United States and other areas of the world adjacent to Western-based universities, a bonanza can be reaped in the form of free marketing assistance by those entrepreneurs who have the acumen to make contact with the marketing departments of local universities and business schools.

This is considerably different from the internship programs explained in Chapter 5. The concept is simple and the potential assistance significant. Many college professors, particularly professors of marketing, continuously seek real world projects to which they can assign their students.

When I was a junior at the University of Connecticut majoring in marketing, one of my independent study courses involved assisting a local business in defining its market and trade radius and devising penetration strategies. I worked with this company for about six weeks, with three to five hours of on-site assistance per week and off-site preparation and follow-up. My reward was a letter grade—I got an A—and the satisfaction of knowing that what I had learned in college definitely was applicable in the real world. The entrepreneur with whom I worked got a rookie marketing consultant at no cost who was able to provide strategies that he admitted he would not have been able to devise on his own.

The fastest way to obtain a roster of marketing professors with potential interest in supplying qualified students to aid in your business is to contact the American Marketing Association at 250 South Wacker Drive, Chicago, IL 60603, (312) 648-0536. For a fee of $100 you can obtain the AMA's membership directory, which cross indexes all members by organization and geography. Thus, you can readily pinpoint the closest universities, employing association members. As an alternative, you can join the AMA and receive the directory free as a benefit of membership. Inquire about membership at the same address above.

Students are particularly adept at conducting survey research, something that you pay dearly for when contracting a professional marketing research firm. Using marketing students you are able to obtain traffic counts, undertake telephone and sight-and-area surveys, study the competition, and assess the potential market demand for new products or services. You initially may be leery of having a team of bright 21-year-olds working as consultants to your business, but after meeting and working with them, I guarantee your fears will quickly vanish.

These marketing students enjoy the opportunity to get out of the classroom and apply what they have learned to a real business that can use their help. To take advantage of this ultra-effective shoestring marketing technique, start making some phone calls.

2. Getting Free Publicity Photos Through Civic Group and Trade Association Memberships

In Chapter 10 we looked at ways of taking advantage of the lunch and dinner circuit by joining targeted groups and prospecting for leads. It is likely that you need photos of yourself on a periodic basis, and not just head and shoulders, but action shots of you in the community. One way to leverage your membership in civic and trade associations is to take advantage of those times in which a photographer will be present. Fortunately, these are identifiable in advance.

Simply call the publicity chairperson, membership director, or meeting planner to find out when the association has scheduled a photographer to take pictures. Usually you can count on at least the annual meeting, any type of awards dinner, and any time a renowned speaker will be lecturing.

Once you have identified the event at which a photographer will be present, obtain the name, address, and phone number of said photographer. Then call and say that you would like to have some photos taken of yourself before or after the association booking.

Why is this an effective shoestring marketing technique? Surprise! In most cases, the photographer won't charge you a sitting fee. The photographer has to be at the event, anyway, and always has more film on hand than is necessary, so taking a couple more shots represents no burden. You gain the perfect setting for the type of action photo you need to enhance your image as a prosperous entrepreneur in the community. You will be all dressed up in a well-lit ballroom or convention center with appropriate backdrops.

I have used this technique on several occasions resulting in some gem photos. Sometimes you get clunkers. But in any case, the time, energy, and expense of duplicating these events simply would not be worth it to most entrepreneurs, and I suspect wouldn't be worth it to you.

3. Publishing Your Own Newsletter

Much has been written on desktop publishing, producing a newsletter, and disseminating information to customer databases in recent years, so I will not reiterate what you may already know. However, if you have never distributed a newsletter, it is probably time to take advantage of available technology. Many of the word processing support businesses in your community now offer desktop publishing. Thus, you don't have to invest in the equipment, learn the software, or go through the agony of having columns that don't line up, typos, etc.

Farming out your newsletter, which can consist of as little as one sheet of paper with copy on both sides, qualifies as a shoestring marketing technique for the simple reason that every time you provide your targeted market niche with literature and information of value to them, you enhance your overall marketing efforts.

Newsletters serve many purposes, according to G.A. Marken, president of Marken Communications in Palo Alto, California, including:

☐ Making readers more aware of your company, its products, and services.

☐ Building interest in your products or services.

☐ Explaining why your customers are satisfied.

☐ Describing various uses for your products and services.

☐ Giving prospects information, through edited testimonials, that shows your products and services deliver as advertised.

☐ Keeping readers informed of the trends, product developments and enhancements, and additional services.

☐ Showing that your organization is working to provide better products and services to the market.

Marken goes on to comment that you should "remove any copy your clients or customers would not be willing to listen to in person." He also advises ensuring that your newsletter is written in a "friendly, almost conversational manner. This style means that you can be approached. A stilted or formal style puts people off."

"If you publish a newsletter," says Marken, "don't try to compete with business trade and consumer publications. Focus on news and information that will assist and educate your customers and the prospect to whom you want to sell. A well edited and produced newsletter—this does not have to mean it is expensive—can improve relations with existing and prospective customers. It can also lead to immediate and direct sales."

After attending one of my lectures, Christine Goon, CPA, added me to the mailing list for her simple newsletter consisting of no more than one sheet with double column typeset copy on both sides of the paper. Christine bills herself as the consultant's accountant, and thus distributes her newsletter to consultants in her area. Because the cost of running off additional copies of the newsletter is negligible once it has already been set in type, Christine and other entrepreneurs like her can afford to send newsletters not only to existing clients and prospects but to additional targets with whom they feel there is business potential.

You probably already have received these types of newsletters, so I won't include a sample. The point is that even if you have never considered this marketing technique before, there has never been a better time than the present to begin.

4. Aiding Millions of Functional Illiterates

I wish the situation weren't true, but by some estimates there are more than 27 million adults in the United States who would have extreme difficulty reading this sentence, not to mention the product or service literature that you have available. But reality being what it is, as an entrepreneur in today's society you have to consider the impact on your business of not being able to appeal to customers because they can't read. So, depending on the nature of your business, it may be good for you to reevaluate your product labels and instructions, sales literature, and other printed information designed to attract new customers and clients.

Are there ways to use pictures or symbols that are worth a thousand words? Open up the Sunday supplement that you usually throw away, and carefully notice the department store, drug store, and appliance store graphics. A color photograph or a carefully drawn sketch accompanies most or all of the products being advertised. Even in a 100 % functionally literate society, photos and graphics help sales, because they allow people to get your message in a hurry. In this age of information overload, many people appreciate being able to get your message quickly and easily without doing a lot of reading.

5. Customer or Client of the Month Award

One super-effective technique that has been used for years is to sponsor a customer or client of the month—or week, if you are very ambitious. This can be done by simply rotating selection among your key customers or clients, finding out a little about their background, and then giving them a plaque they can display. Meanwhile, a duplicate of the plaque is posted on your premises. Naturally you issue a press release to the local paper, take the customer or client's picture and create a mini event.

I have seen health clubs that sponsor a member of the month profile, delicatessens that have a customer of the week (based on the single largest cash register ring-up), and other businesses that find similar excuses to honor their customers or clients.

Another strategy on this theme is to offer a good citizen award to someone in the community who may not even be one of your customers or clients. Simply read the local newspaper and see who did something that supported civic or community interests, or solicit input from your customers and clients. As your award program begins to gain recognition, people automatically will volunteer names of individuals, including themselves, and you can parlay this into publicity.

The long-term effect of this type of award program is that you build excellent goodwill among existing customers and clients. If you post the award plaque or photo, you can begin generating a local "mini celebrity" wall. Naturally, this wall will be frequented by those on it. It also will generate long standing customer interest and establish you as a fixture within the community.

6. Posting Autographed Celebrity Photos

Walk into Michael O'Harro's sports bar, Champions, in the Georgetown section of Washington, DC, and you will immediately be knocked off your feet by the number of autographed pictures he has of baseball, football, basketball, and other sports heroes. O'Harro found a way to fill every wall, nook and cranny in Champions with sports trivia and autographed photos, and this has helped his saloon to become one of the local tourist spots that everyone simply must see.

You can practice a variation on this theme by sending $9.45 to Michael Levine at 9123 Sunset Boulevard, Los Angeles, CA 90069 to obtain a copy of *The New Address Book*. This book contains the names and addresses of celebrities, sports figures, politicians, and authors throughout the world. In most cases the address provided is that of the celebrity's agent or representative. But for your purposes that is just fine. You simply write to the agent requesting an autographed photo. In some cases they are available for a nominal fee through the agent, and in other cases they are available from the celebrity's fan club. That address can be provided by the agent.

· In a short time you, too, can have photos of Sylvester Stallone, Sally Fields, and Jack Nicholson adorning your walls. Then everyone can marvel at the charm and appeal that your business must have in order to attract such world renowned celebrities. If you are interested in photos of politicians, statesmen, and ambassadors, try writing to them in Washington, DC in care of their press agents. Most senators and congressmen can be reached by addressing the letter to them in care of the United States Congress, Washington, DC 20515. You only need a handful of these photos before the legends about *you* start to grow.

7. Customer-Related News Angles

If you are a retail entrepreneur or a business or professional service provider, you can parlay client or customer news into a feature story in your local paper. In many instances, the key to ensuring that a reporter will call you is to get the customer to make the initial call to the reporter.

□ A customer is instrumental in helping to solve a crime, either by recalling details or by providing you or authorities with key information that leads to its solution. Naturally, you reward the customer with some type of gift.

□ The 1,000th, 10,000th, 100,000th, or 1,000,000th customer passes through your doors. In order to take maximum advantage of this, prepare a news release in advance and leave appropriate blanks for the name of the customer, whoever he or she turns out to be. Then submit this yourself to the local press along with a photo. It's a "can't miss" proposition.

□ Ask one of your key clients or customers to call a reporter and suggest that you offer the best _____ in the community and that they ought to come out to the store/office/plant and observe for themselves firsthand the best kept secret in town.

☐ Donate your premises for some civic or charitable group meeting that the media will attend. At the very least, any report of the meeting will include the line, "... the meeting, held last night at the ABCD company...."

☐ If you or one of your customers stumbles upon a use for your product or service that is somewhat offbeat, wacky, or exciting, suggest that your customer call the local reporter covering your "beat." Reporters need to produce interesting copy as much as you want to be in print.

☐ Always be on the lookout for a way to tie your product or service to some currently breaking news item. Back during the Iran-Contra Affair hearings a seminar leader who offered courses on business and professional ethics circulated a news release that was widely published. Courses on ethics are nothing new, so why did this particular story become popular so quickly? His theme was "Fawn Hall [secretary to Lt. Col. Oliver North] Wouldn't Have Shredded Top Secret Documents If She Had Taken a Course on Ethics." This type of promotional strategy can spread like wildfire if you are the first to parlay some late-breaking news event into a press release that highlights the products or services you have to offer. In order to take advantage of this vehicle, simply turn on the news this evening or read the newspaper.

8. Establish a Customer Resource Center

A well-stocked display case with brochures about products you sell can be an important marketing tool. If you sell equipment, brochures describing how to use the equipment safely and effectively are great marketing aids.

If you own a professional services firm, brochures describing the range of services you offer and featuring testimony from previous clients can pay off well. Books about other firms offering services complementary to yours also could be helpful to customers. Dentists' and doctors' offices frequently have cases displaying four or five brochures on diseases or treatments about which people frequently have questions. If you order the brochures from an outside firm, be sure to have your name, address, and phone number imprinted on the brochures. Most have a blank for such information.

9. Small Is Beautiful When It's Repeated Enough

Have you ever noticed the same small ad repeated frequently in a newspaper or magazine? This is a good example of effective, inexpensive advertising. Big is not always better! A series of 8, 10, or 12 similar small ads can be equally or even more productive than a large ad, and it costs less overall.

This is especially applicable with small ads. A well-placed series of small ads helps build long-term recognition and target awareness. A series should always appear in the same location, so that readers will notice it each time. You must hit appropriate readers. If those seeing your ad are not the right target market, your efforts will be wasted.

10. Long Distance Calling at Off Peak Hours

A couple times a month, between 9 A.M. and 11 A.M., I get calls from clients or business associates in California. These callers realize that at 6 A.M. to 8 A.M. Pacific Coast time, long-distance calls, irrespective of whose system you are using, cost much less than after 8 A.M. Conversely, when you make marketing, sales or other calls to the West Coast or to the Mid-West, if you are not waiting till 5:05 P.M. to make your calls and have not instructed your staff to do the same, you are pouring dollars down the phone line.

11. Free Nationwide Telephone Advisory Service

Bob Bly is the founder and director of the Advertising Hotline based in New Milford, New Jersey. He is also a prolific author, having written 14 books including *The Copywriter's Handbook* (New York: Dodd Mead, 1985) and *Create the Perfect Sales Piece* (New York: Wiley, 1985). Bob also initiated a unique program to help business professionals and, at the same time, to generate prospecting leads for his own consulting services. The card in Figure 12-1 says it all.

> For free information, tips, and advice call . . .
> ## ☎ The Advertising Hotline ™
> ## 201-599-2276
> FREE nationwide telephone advisory service for
> Advertising • Direct Marketing • Promotion • Publicity
>
> A 24-hour hotline   Bob Bly, Director
>   (201) 599-2277

Figure 12-1. The Advertising Hotline offers useful free information. Reprinted with the permission of Bob Bly.

By calling Bob on the "Advertising Hotline," anyone can get free information.

Reflect for a moment on the products and services that you offer. Would it be worth the time and trouble to offer a free hotline? This is a high leverage, low-cost marketing technique because those dialing you pay for the call. Your investment consists largely of producing a business card, a preprinted Rolodex card, or supporting literature to get the word out that your service is available. Then you only need to build some flexibility into your schedule so that you or your staff can handle phone calls throughout the work week.

Bob offers a 24-hour hotline; however, being available on a more restricted basis also can be effective.

12. Telephone Consultation for a Monthly Fee

The Montgomery Ward Company, known for selling appliances, housewares, and clothing, recently introduced a new service for its customers. For $6.75 per month, Montgomery Ward will provide unlimited phone and mail consultations with a lawyer. Over 200,000 people have subscribed to this service. The Amway Corporation, known for its health foods, cleaning products, and other household goods, recently began offering a similar legal package. And Hyatt Legal Services, headquartered in Kansas City, offers a $10 a month "law plan" for Citibank credit card holders.

What type of consultation service can you offer to either your existing customers or another targeted market? Is your product knowledge or professional background such that additional revenue could be generated by signing up customers to pay a monthly fee for advice?

To test the waters for this marketing venture, much as with Bob Bly's free hotline service, you need only produce a simple flyer for insertion with normal correspondence to existing customers and for distribution at your place of business and with other mailings.

The reason why Montgomery Ward Legal Advice and other competitive systems work so well is that people want and need professional legal advice but often are hesitant to retain lawyers for fear of high prices. By offering an information service for a small monthly fee, you reduce many of the fears of those needing the type of consultation you can offer.

Such a program works very well for personal computer consultants. A Greensboro, North Carolina consultant was able to attract 18 subscribers at $11.50 per month in his very first month of operation. He sent a simple one-page flyer to the names on his mailing list and asked customers and friends to tell others about his service. In a few months, the program became so popular that he hired an assistant and expanded his office.

Naturally, subscribers will have need for additional services beyond those that can be offered over the telephone. With both the legal and personal computer consultation programs, considerable additional business is derived.

13. Promoting New Uses for Your Products and Services

Depending on your product or service, discovering alternative uses for it may take some imagination. However, this may yield new opportunities to reach your target market. For example, petroleum jelly was first promoted as a gel to heal burns or damaged skin. Later it was touted as a skin conditioner. In the past couple of years, television commercials have extolled its virtues as a make-up remover.

Similarly, baking soda has gone through numerous repositioning evolutions. At various times it has been promoted as dentifrice, carpet cleaner, cat litter box deodorant, and refrigerator freshener. When evaluating your product(s), consider the opportunities. Can your product be:

□ Combined with something else?

□ Made to do different jobs?

□ Packaged more attractively?

□ Produced at a lighter weight?

□ Easier to clean?

□ Enlarged?

□ Reused?

□ Less expensive?

□ Faster?

□ Portable?

There also are numerous ways to look at the services you provide. For example, temporary service firms traditionally placed secretaries and receptionists. Many firms now place accountants, graphic artists, editors, and managers.

Promoting a new use for your services enables you to build on your existing base and try new marketing approaches on limited capital. Your name and services are already known among a target market, so you are trading on their positive connotations. If the strategy doesn't work, you haven't lost much.

Here are some suggestions for reassessing your service offering:

□ Can you provide printed instructions?

□ Will customer follow-up increase perceived value?

□ Can you cut costs or materials and still provide the same service?

□ Can you perform some aspect of the service at the client's site?

□ Can it be done in less time?

□ Can you offer peripherals or accessories?

□ Would renaming it increase its value?

14. Widening Your Pool of Prospects

Prospects for your business are all around you, although many of the people you already know or encounter are never considered as such. Insurance agents have long known the secret of clipping newspaper notification of births, newcomers to town, and newlyweds. Financial brokers generate clients from "names in the news," professional directories, and magazine articles.

Your task of identifying new prospects need not be that difficult. For example, suppliers, creditors, and all those with whom you do business are likely candidates. Your doctor, dentist, lawyer, hairdresser, and accountant are all fair game when it comes to widening your pool of prospects. So are the people who populate the organizations to which you belong—from the PTA to the Elks to a local church group. Don't forget the contacts and organizations of your spouse, children, friends, and relatives.

Anyone who targets you as a prospect must be evaluated by you as a prospect for your business. This may not always work, but it is an instant and regular way to keep your "prospecting juices" flowing. Finally, tap the personal contacts of your employees. Let them know that you actively seek, appreciate, and give credit for names of individuals or businesses that may have need for your products or services.

When you think about it, prospects are all around you all the time.

15. Using "Words That Sell"

Richard Bayan has written a wonderful little book, *Words That Sell* (Westbury, NY: Asher-Gallant, 1984) in which he offers lists of phrases that you can use to market your business. For example, one section, "Heads and Slogans," offers such bouncy starters as:

> Get comfortable with _____
> Break away from the pack with _____
> Your partner in _____
> There is no substitute for _____
> Get hooked on _____
> They don't call us _____ for nothing

Another section, "Opening with a Question," offers such lines as:

Want to keep in touch with _____?
Who could say no to _____ ?
Will you be ready for the _____ ?
Don't you wish _____ ?
How can you cut the high cost of _____ ?
Are you just a little curious about _____ ?

The book continues on with "Opening with a Challenge," "Salutations and Invitations," "Authentic," "Complete/Thorough," "Persuading the Reader" (see Figure 12-2), "Making Contact," and "Discounts/Sales." Dozens of readily usable examples are provided in each section.

When I first came across this book I immediately used it because it offered a quick, no-cost way to begin producing my own copy. Even when I don't use any of the phrases provided in *Words That Sell*, it is valuable as an idea stimulator and invariably hastens the rate at which I do produce the phrase I was looking for.

16. From Customer Evaluation to Marketing Lead

Dynacolor Graphics Incorporated of Miami, Florida has a unique customer evaluation form, shown in Figure 12-3. The company's president, Donald M. Duncanson, offers a personal appeal to customers, stating in bold letters, "We need your help!" The first part of Dynacolor's evaluation form asks standard questions relating to company performance. The second page asks customers:

☐ How did they distribute the materials that Dynacolor produced for them?
☐ What were the results?
☐ What are the plans regarding these items in the future?
☐ Do they have any special needs?

The evaluation form ends with a section that asks if it is okay for Dynacolor to quote comments supplied by the customer and to use the customer's name.

Combining customer evaluation and marketing leads on the same form is an excellent example of shoestring marketing. Cus-

Persuading the Reader

Why settle for _____ when you can have _____?

You'll want to add it to your personal collection.

_____ belongs in the home of every educated family.

You'll receive all these benefits:

You can't lose.

What have you got to lose?

In short, you've got nothing to lose.

This is the opportunity you've been waiting for.

A rewarding _____ awaits you.

Can you think of any reason *not* to send for your _____?

You owe it to your family to...

Frankly, I can't understand why *everybody* doesn't take advantage of this offer.

We think you'll find that...

We think you'll agree...

We stand behind our claims.

We're ready to prove everything we claim.

When every dollar counts, it's good to know that...

Your gift is tax-deductible.

I know you receive appeals from many good causes, but I can't think of a better cause than...

We need you...you need us!

Does all this sound too good to be true?

You'll still be able to do it your way—only better!

Before you buy a _____, find out what _____ has to offer.

You'll wonder how you ever managed without it.

We're sure to have the perfect _____ for you.

You won't be disappointed.

Put your _____ to the test.

Seeing is believing.

That's all it takes to...

All this can be yours.

Take as many as you wish—or none at all!

You can see for yourself that...

Once you try us, you'll want to stay with us.

Our supply is limited.

In the last analysis, all that matters is...

Remember, time is running out.

Take advantage of this special offer.

You'll be glad you did.

Try to imagine the alternative.

Think of what you have to look forward to!

Figure 12-2. A selection of useful phrases and slogans from *Words That Sell*. Reprinted with the permission of the author.

tomers automatically receive this form after Dynacolor Graphics completes a job for them. As with most surveys, many customers don't respond. Those who do are providing Dynacolor with high quality marketing information from which the company is able to make forecasts, provide detailed customer follow-up, refine quality control procedures, and minimize customer grievances.

dynacolor
graphics, inc.®

1182 N.W. 159th Drive
Miami, Florida 33169
305/625-5388

Job Number	
Product	
Title	
Size	
Quantity	
Representative	

Name _____

Firm Name _____

Address _____

City _____ State _____ Zip _____

You are a valued customer and Dynacolor wants to keep it that way!

How did we do? Was the job printed for you up to your expectations? Was it produced on schedule? Give it to us straight because we want to correct any short-comings and be able to print for you in the future.

Thanks for your cooperation.

Donald M. Duncanson

Donald M. Duncanson
President

CUSTOMER'S EVALUATION AND SUGGESTIONS

YOUR APPRAISAL... good, bad or otherwise. Tell it like it is!

☐ YES   Did Dynacolor produce the quality of
☐ No   full color printing you expected?
Comment:

☐ Yes   Was the job printed and delivered on
☐ No   schedule?
Comment:

☐ Yes   Did Dynacolor people give you good
☐ No   service and cooperation?
Comment:

☐ Yes   Will you come back to Dynacolor for
☐ No   full color printing?
Comment:

_____
_____
_____
_____
_____
_____
_____
_____

Figure 12-3. A customer evaluation form like this one can serve many marketing purposes. Reprinted with the permission of Dynacolor graphics.

197

MARKETING INFORMATION

To serve you and all Dynacolor customers better, we need the following marketing research information . . . we want to pass on your ideas and suggestions. Your cooperation will be appreciated.

(1) HOW USED

DISTRIBUTED VIA:

- [ ] U.S. MAIL
- [ ] HANDOUTS
- [ ] PICK-UPS
- [ ] ENCLOSURES
- [ ] SALES PEOPLE
- [ ] SHOWS/CONVENTIONS
- [ ] OTHER:

Brief description of uses:

(2) RESULTS / BENEFITS

- [ ] Results about as expected!
- [ ] Results better than expected!
- [ ] Results less than expected!

Details on results (figures if possible).

(3) FUTURE USE PLANS

- [ ] Will reprint and use again!
- [ ] Will use similar job in the future.
- [ ] Will use different promotion piece!

(4) SPECIAL NEEDS

- [ ] I have special needs and want samples and ideas. (Explain:)

(5)

- [ ] OK for Dynacolor to quote my comments.
- [ ] OK to use my personal name.
- [ ] Do not use my name.
- [ ] OK to use company name.
- [ ] Do not use company name.

Signed _____ Date _____

Figure 12.3 (continued)

198

Many companies are afraid to put themselves on the line, to ask customers if the results received were less than expected or if they would return with other jobs. But Dynacolor and companies like it are in business for the long haul. They strive to maintain integrity in the products and services offered. They recognize the need to stay close to the customer, and they understand that customer service and marketing go hand in hand.

APPENDIX

A SHOESTRING MARKETER'S GRAND OPENING PLAN

The key to a successful grand opening of a new office is to stimulate interest among key business and community leaders prior to the actual opening. This requires that several steps be taken well in advance.

July

1. As soon as the new name is established, print business cards and stationery. A rubber stamp or a set of gummed labels also should be prepared, giving information about the grand opening.
2. Request listings or purchase space in the Yellow Pages, the Blue Book, mini phone directories, and other directories serving the local area.
3. Be sure that all advertising and promotional literature includes an aerial map indicating the precise location of the office.
4. Prepare a variety of public announcements and press releases to be submitted one or two weeks prior to the opening. A sample public announcement would be as follows:

"ABC Group announces its grand opening in the Johnson Building in Bloomfield on _____ 1988. The principal, Edmund Harris, has had 12 years of experience servicing the greater Bloomfield area. Appointments will be taken, starting on the 15th of September."

This type of announcement should have on its reverse side a detailed map, drawn to scale, indicating the precise location of the new office in relation to Park Place, the bus stop, and other readily identifiable landmarks.

Press releases should be written on a variety of topics, including the hiring of new personnel, additional services and facilities, the convenient and timely service you'll be providing to business executives, etc.

5. Pay a visit to the Bloomfield Business Center or Chamber of Commerce to obtain information on seminars and club meetings that will be held in the area in the coming two months. Similar information can be obtained by closely examining the business section of the Morning Times. Attend as many Bloomfield business functions as possible so that key connections can be made. The fact that your new office is opening in a convenient location is welcome news to many of the people you'll be meeting.

6. Be sure to write to your college alumni newspaper and inform them of the new office. Undoubtedly, several alumni are in the Bloomfield area.

August

1. Prepare invitations for your grand opening, to be distributed to all businesses in your building, and surrounding hotels and executive office buildings. Hire a college student to distribute these cards throughout the Bloomfield area.

2. Have a secretary or receptionist begin calling all the hotels in the area to get the names of the managers. At the end of August, personally visit each of these managers and propose the following plan: Offer your services to hotel and motel guests in Bloomfield for business or vacation. Be sure to leave plenty of announcement cards with maps, and suggest that the manager include the cards in the hotel lobby and room literature, which guests frequently peruse.

In actuality, few guests ever call to use your services via this promotional strategy. The hotel and motel managers and staff often end up using your services because they've read the message so often.

3. Begin developing a strategy to offer *special executive service.* While this service is nothing more than what you usually provide, business executives will respond to such a campaign. This enables you to offer quick turnaround service or guaranteed starting or

ending times to executives who are willing to pay five to ten dollars more per visit. This special executive service strategy is one that generates good word of mouth—satisfied business executives will tell others to ask for the special executive service at your office.

4. Visit the manager of the fast food restaurant nearby and ask if there's any promotional tie-in that you might arrange. The fast food franchisers are known for their local promotion capabilities. They will not pass up the opportunity to achieve a synergistic effect. The tie-in must, of course, be something that you believe is beneficial to all concerned.

5. In addition to announcements that will be hand-delivered, you may wish to do a mass mailing of the area, including business and residential addresses. To do this, you may purchase the mailing list of the Bloomfield Review (newsletter), any of the other area newspapers, and newsletters.

6. Call all of the area condominium and high-rise building managers and ask for copies of their newsletters. They may refer you to a publication manager. State that you're contemplating advertising in the newsletter, and they will be more than happy to supply you with samples and helpful suggestions.

September

1. Understaff your office for as long as possible. Use part-time help. New full-time personnel can be added when necessary. Having several people on the payroll who are not being fully utilized for several weeks can be quite costly.

2. Issue new press releases to the local papers five to seven days before the actual opening.

3. Place at least two listings in your building directory in the main lobby. For example, you should be listed as JKL Offices, Edmund Harris and as Edmund Harris, JKL Offices.

4. Secure permission from the building rental agent and/or manager to distribute literature, handouts, balloons, buttons, etc., in the hallway during the grand opening week or just after the grand opening.

5. Seven to ten days before opening, have phones installed so that appointments can be scheduled. If all the announcements and business cards distributed thus far contain a sticker or stamp

indicating that appointments will be taken at such and such a time, it's important that a voice be at the other end of the phone number listed.

6. Have employees visit all of the offices in your building, reminding them about the open house two or three days before actual occurrence.

7. Begin the open house at 5 P.M. Have all employees ready to greet guests. A modest but well-selected offering of wine and hors d'oeuvres will do nicely. During the open house, feel free to talk business.

8. Collect business cards in a bowl, perhaps offering a door prize.

9. Prepare announcement cards urging people to tell their friends about the new office. Then, as correspondents increase, double the value of all mail you send by including the "Tell Your Friends" card.

10. Post a message on all community bulletin boards in the area. *A two- or three-hour* comprehensive walk will be necessary.

Optional Activities Concurrent with Start-Up

1. Participate in the local value pack, in which your advertisement and perhaps a discount coupon are offered to thousands of residents in the area via direct mail.

2. Seek reciprocal promotional courtesies. This involves individually visiting each of the nearby merchants and discussing how you may help one another's business.

3. When any of the staff makes a trip to other business establishments in Bloomfield, such as restaurants or banks, have them take some office announcement cards to leave in strategically located places. For example, leave them near the teller's window at the bank, on the check-out counter at the dry cleaners, in restaurant foyers, etc.

4. Use your industry's brochures to your advantage. Hereafter stamp them with your address and indicate that your office is the local distributor of such information.

5. Start a good citizen award. Each week clip from the paper news of someone who performed a good deed for another person or

the community in general. Set up a program asking people to make nominations for the award. They'll begin sending letters telling of good deeds that others have performed, and each week you can choose the best of these. Take a picture of the winner and describe what they did in order to be awarded the plaque. You can get newspaper coverage for at least the first award with the story about your program.

BIBLIOGRAPHY

BOOKS

Baber, Michael F. *Integrated Business Leadership through Cross-Marketing.* St. Louis: Green, 1986.

Bayan, Richard. *Words That Sell.* Westbury, NY: Asher-Gallant Press, 1984.

Bedrosian, Margaret M. *Speak Like a Pro.* New York: Wiley, 1986.

Connor, Richard A. Jr., and Jeffrey P. Davidson. *Marketing Your Consulting and Professional Services.* New York: Wiley, 1985.

Connor, Richard A. Jr., and Jeffrey P. Davidson. *Getting New Clients.* New York: Wiley, 1987.

Davidson, Jeffrey P. *Marketing to the Fortune 500.* Homewood, IL: Dow Jones-Irwin, 1987.

Evans, Joel R., and Berry Berman. *Marketing,* 2nd ed. New York: Macmillan, 1985.

Gershman, Michael. *Smarter Barter: A Guide for Corporations, Professionals in Small Business.* New York: Viking, 1986.

Gschwandtner, Gerhard. *How to Become a Master Sales Builder.* Englewood Cliffs, NJ: Prentice-Hall, 1987.

Krimmins, Ed. *Cooperative Advertising.* New York: Wolfe, 1985.

Ries, Al, and Jack Trout. *Positioning: The Battle for Your Mind.* New York: McGraw-Hill, 1981.

ARTICLES

Alessandra, Dr. Tony, and Jim Cathcart. "Qualities of the Professional Sales Person." *Marketing Communications,* December, 1985, p. 132.

Bellizzi, Kathy, and Mona Piontkowski. "What Is in a Brochure?" *Training Magazine,* February 1987, p. 58.

"Commerce Publishes Guide to Countertrade." *Business America,* February 4, 1985, p. 35.

Dolen, Michael. "Creating Effective Logos with Word Graphics." *Business Marketing,* December 1984, p. 92.

Dunlap, Bill. "Taking a Reading of the Yellow Pages." *Marketing and Media Decisions*, Fall 1985 Special, p. 85.

Everett, Martin. "A Force in the Field." *Sales and Marketing Management*, May 13, 1985, p. 82.

Flax, Steven. "Worldwinds Hit the Yellow Pages." *Fortune*, October 1, 1984, p. 113.

Fletcher, Allen D. "Boosting Yellow Pages Impact." *Communications Briefing*, June 1986.

Granrose, Cherlyn S., and Eileen Applebaum. "The Efficiency of Temporary Help in Part-Time Employment." *Personnel Administrator*, January 1986, p. 71.

"How to Create Great Yellow Pages Ads." American Association of Yellow Page Publishers, 1986.

Jackson, Ralph, and A. Parasuraman. "The Yellow Pages Is an Advertising Tool for Small Businesses." *American Journal of Small Business*, Spring 1986, p. 29.

Koten, John. "Upheaval in Middle Class Market Forces Changing in Selling Strategies." *Wall Street Journal*, March 13, 1987, p. 27.

Lewis, Ray. "Co-op: A Coup for Greater Profits." *Marketing Communications*, September 1985, p. 66.

Marken, G. A. "Newsletters Are a Good Way to Build Sales." *Marketing News*, November 7, 1986, p. 4.

"MCI to Ring In 800 Service Ten Percent Below AT&T's Tolls." *Wall Street Journal*, February 13, 1987, p. 14.

Much, Marilyn. "Swap Cameras for Bananas?" *Industry Week*, October 13, 1986, p. 76.

Reiling, Lynn G. "Countertrade Revives 'Dead Goods.'" *Marketing News*, August 29, 1986, p. 1.

"Return on Investment: Look at the Effectiveness of Yellow Pages Advertising." American Association of Yellow Page Publishers, 1986.

Richter, Paul. "Firms Strike Gold in the Yellow Pages." *Los Angeles Times*, July 12, 1985.

Salone, Pat. "Wrangle Back to Basics with Willie." *Advertising Age*, December 2, 1985, p. 99.

"Seeking Out Part-Timers." *Management World*, November 1984, p. 24.

"Spokesdude Speaks Lingo of Auto Buffs in Purolator Promotion." *Marketing News*, September 26, 1986, p. 11.

"Three Florida 'Environments' Team Marketing." *Marketing News*, April 25, 1986.

Tucker, Elizabeth. "Advertisers Seeing Red as Yellow Pages Multiply." *Washington Post: Washington Business*, March 16, 1987, p. 1.

"What the Boom and Part-Time Work Means for Management." *Industry Week*, May 1984, p. 38.

GLOSSARY

Action letter – A targeted letter, sent on President's stationery, to a client or prospect suggesting that you meet to discuss a new product or service idea.

Advertising – Any paid form of non-personal presentation of ideas, goods or services by an identified sponsor. The main form of mass selling.

Barter – The exchange of goods and services between parties in lieu of cash.

Business association – Business owners and managers in close proximity who have joined together to achieve synergistic results, particularly in the areas of advertising, insurance, maintenance, and security.

Business service – Enterprises engaged in rendering cleaning, maintenance, repair, installation, removal, and similar services to other businesses and consumers.

Client – Those who use or have used a professional service.

Co-operative advertising – An arrangement whereby a national manufacturer or distributor pays for a portion of the local advertising sponsored by a business.

Countertrade – Various commercial practices in which exports of goods or services are linked to reciprocal exchanges, thus reducing or eliminating net cash payments. Barter is the simplest and oldest form of countertrade.

Customer – Business patrons buying its products and services. The primary factor and most crucial element in the existence of a business. A person or group with potentially unmet needs.

Customer service – Satisfying and assisting consumers by various means including offering technical assistance, handling grievances, providing information, and making substitutions.

Demographics – An analysis of the characteristics, traits, and buying patterns of a targeted population.

Direct mail – A form of advertising in which a message is sent to pre-selected targets.

Distribution channel – The set of parties assisting in transferring particular goods or services from producer to consumer.

Entrepreneur – An individual who conceives or converts a product or service that fulfills a need in the marketplace.

Forecasting – The art of anticipating both what amount of revenue will be generated in a given time period and what buyers are likely to do under a given set of conditions.

***Fortune* 500** – The 500 largest U.S. industrial corporations based on sales volume. Tabulated and ranked by *Fortune* magazine.

Geographic segmentation – Subdividing a market into units such as continents, nations, states, regions, counties, cities, or neighborhoods.

Good faith – Acting with a sincere belief that the accomplishment intended is not unlawful or harmful to another.

Goodwill – Intangible assets of a firm established by the amount of the price paid for the going concern above book value.

Image – The sum total of all the perceptions your customers, clients, and all others have about you and your business.

Interns – Students who work outside the university classroom for a letter grade and/or nominal fee. Arranged by the university and employers.

Internship – A program over a prescribed period of time in which an intern works or provides service for a letter grade and/or nominal fee.

Leverage – The identification and use of relatively limited resources in order to achieve disproportionate gain.

Leveraging – The process of identifying and capitalizing on the smallest number of actions which produce the largest number/amount of results.

Market – The set of existing and prospective users of a product or service.

Marketing – The process of planning and executing the conception, pricing, promotion, and distribution of ideas, goods and services to create exchanges that satisfy individual and organizational objectives.

Marketing information system – A network of people, equipment, and procedures to collect organize, analyze, evaluate, and distribute timely, relevant, and accurate information used by marketing decision makers.

Marketing management – The analysis, planning, implementation, and control of programs designed to create, build and maintain mutually beneficial exchanges with target buyers for the purpose of achieving organizational objectives.

Marketing plan – The "hard-copy" end-product of the marketing planning process.

Marketing planning – The continuing process of: auditing the company and its markets to identify opportunities and problems; establishing priority; setting goals; allocating and organizing resources required to accomplish the goals; and scheduling, doing, and monitoring results.

Marketing research – The systematic collection, analysis, and reporting of data to provide information for marketing decision making.

Marketing strategy – The marketing logic by which a business seeks to achieve its marketing objectives.

Market penetration – A systematic campaign to increase sales in current markets of an existing product or service.

Market segment – A distinct or definable subset of a target market.

Marketing vehicle – That which is used in support of one's marketing plan and marketing strategies.

Niche – (or marketing niche) an identifiable market or market segment which can be readily and prosperously penetrated.

Overhead – All the costs of business other than direct labor and materials, including such items as maintenance, supervision, utility costs, and depreciation.

Personal selling – A professional marketing effort involving face-to-face communication and feedback, with the goal of making a sale or inducing a favorable attitude towards a company and its product or services.

Press release – An announcement of community, state, national, or international interest distributed to print media by the organization for and about whom the announcement is written.

Product – Product or services that can be offered to a market for acquisition, use, consumption, or adoption that satisfies a want or need.

Product differentiation – Presenting a product such that it is perceived by customers as unique or somewhat unique from other products available.

Product line – A group of products that are closely related because they satisfy a class of needs, are used together, are sold to the same customer groups, are marketed through the same type of outlet, or fall within given price ranges. Also can mean the full range of products marketed by a company.

Product mix – The set of all product lines and items that a particular seller offers to buyers.

Professional service – Businesses engaged in rendering advice, consultation, assistance, support, or specific results for a fee, usually on a retainer or hourly basis.

Promotion – The act of furthering the growth and development of a business by generating exposure of goods or services to a target market.

Prospecting – The activities involved in seeking potential buyers or customers; identifying and contacting likely candidates for purchase of your goods or services.

Psychographics – The art and science of determining consumption patterns and preferences based on identified characteristics of a heterogeneous group.

Purchasing agent – As used here, a general term connotating any employed individual whose job responsibility in some way involves buying goods and/or services.

Reciprocal advertising – Displaying or presenting the commercial message of a business enterprise, who in turn displays your commercial message.

Reference – As used here, a letter or oral testimony from a customer or client stating that your products and/or services were found to be of value.

Referral – As used here, a name provided to you by a customer, client, or other known party, who has the potential to become a customer or client of your business or service. Also the act of others mentioning your name and providing you with introductions to third parties that may lead to new business opportunities.

Reputation – How a business or individual is regarded by customers and others.

Selling – The exchange of goods, services, or ideas between two parties.

Standard Industrial Classification (S.I.C.) – A U.S. Bureau of the Census classification of industries based on the product produced or operation performed by the industry.

Target market – That portion of the total market that a company has selected to serve.

Target marketing – Focusing marketing efforts on one or more segments within a total market.

Telemarketing – A systemized effort employing the telephone to develop new business, service existing accounts, or otherwise aid in the overall marketing process of a business.

Telescript, or telephone script – A written guide used in making telephone contacts.

Test marketing – Selecting one or more markets in which to introduce a new product or service, and observing and assessing what strategy changes are needed, if any.

Tip clubs – Associations of non-competing entrepreneurs who share information with one another about potential clients and customers.

Trade association – An organization established to benefit members of the same trade by informing them of issues and developments within the organization and about how changes outside the organization will affect them.

Vendor – As used here, synonymous with supplier; one who fulfills product or service needs.

Word of mouth – The most effective form of advertising, which occurs when a satisfied customer or client of a business tells one or more other parties.

Working capital – A measure of a firm's short-term assets, including cash, short-term securities, accounts receivable, and inventories, and its ability to meet short-term obligations.

RECOMMENDED READING

Bates, Jefferson D. *Writing with Precision*. Washington, DC: Acropolis Books, 1980.

Bly, Robert W., and Gary Blake. *Technical Writing: Structure, Standards and Style*. New York: McGraw-Hill, 1982.

Bly, Robert W. *The Copywriter's Handbook*. New York: Dodd Mead, 1985.

Bly, Robert W. *Create the Perfect Sales Piece*. New York: Wiley, 1985.

Bruneau, Edmond A. *Prescription for Advertising*. Spokane, WA: Boston Books, 1986.

Burton, Philip W. *Advertising Copywriting*. New York: McGraw-Hill, 1983.

Cananagh, Clifford Y. *The Winning Performance—How America's High Growth Midsize Companies Succeed*. New York: Bantam Books, 1985.

Carnegie, Dale. *How to Win Friends and Influence People, Revised*. New York: Simon & Schuster, 1984.

Church, Nancy J. *Marketing for Nonprofit Cultural Organizations*. Plattsburgh, NY: Clinton-Essex Franklin Library System, 1986.

Cohen, Paula Marantz. *A Public Relations Primer: Thinking and Writing in Context*. Englewood Cliffs, NJ: Prentice-Hall, 1986.

Connor, Tim. *The Soft Sell.* Crofton, MD: T.R. Training Associates, 1981.

Davidson, Jeffrey P. *Avoiding the Pitfalls of Starting Your Own Business*. New York: Walker & Company, 1988.

Deran, Elizabeth. *Low-Cost Marketing Strategies*. Westport, CT: Praeger, 1986.

Fielden, John S., Jean D. Fielden, and Ronald E. Dulek. *The Business Writing Style Book*. Englewood Cliffs, NJ: Prentice-Hall, 1984.

Frankenstein, George, and Diane Frankenstein. *Brandnames: Who Owns What*. New York: Facts on File, 1986.

Geffner, Andrea B. *Business English*. Woodbury, NY: Barron, 1982.

Gondolfo, Joe with Robert L. Shook. *How to Make Big Money Selling*. New York: Harper & Row, 1984.

Hafer, Keith W. and Gordon E. White. *Advertising Writing*. St. Paul, MN: West, 1982.

Kunitskaya-Peterson, Christina. *International Dictionary of Obscenities*. Berkeley, CA: Berkeley Slavic, 1981.

LeBouef, Michael, PhD. *The Greatest Management Principles in the World*. New York: Putnam, 1985.

Ling, Mona. *How to Make Appointments by Telephone*. Englewoods Cliffs, NJ: Prentice-Hall, 1963.

Lumley, James E. A. *Sell It By Mail*. Somerset, NJ: Wiley, 1986.

Malickson, David L., and John W. Nason. *Advertising: How to Write the Kind That Works*. New York: Scribner's, 1982.

McLean, Janice, ed. *1987–88 Consultants & Consulting Organizations Directory–7th Edition*. Detroit: Gale Research, 1986.

Milton, Shirley F., and Arthur A. Winters. *The Creative Connection: Advertising Copy and Idea Visualization*. New York: Fairchild, 1981.

Norins, Hanley. *The Compleat Copywriter: A Comprehensive Guide to All Phases of Advertising Communication*. Melbourne, FL: Krieger, 1980.

Olmsted, Barney, and Suzanne Smith. *The Job-Sharing Handbook*. Alexandria, VA: Association of Part-Time Professionals, 1985.

Parker, Robert B. *Mature Advertising: A Handbook of Effective Advertising Copy*. Reading, MA.: Addison-Wesley, 1981.

Patton, Forrest H. *Force of Persuasion: Dynamic Techniques for Influencing People*. New York: Prentice-Hall, 1986.

Phillips, Michael, and Salli Rasberry. *Marketing Without Advertising*. Berkeley, CA: Nolo Press, 1986.

Prevette, Earl. *How to Increase Sales by Telephone*, C & R Anthony, 1958.

Rothbery, Diane S., and Barbara Ensor Cook. *Part-Time Professional*. Alexandria, VA: Association of Part-Time Professionals, 1985.

Schwab, Victor O. *How to Write a Good Advertisement*. North Hollywood, CA: Wilshire, 1980.

Smith, Cynthia. *How to Get Big Results from a Small Advertising Budget*. New York: Hawthorn Books, 1973.

St. John, Tracy. *Getting Your Public Relations Story on TV and Radio*. Babylon, NY: Pilot Books, 1986.

Thomas, Robert B. *A President's Guide to Developing Sales Strategies*. Los Angeles: Thomas Partners/Adv., 1986.

Toffler, Alvin. *Future Shock*. New York: Morrow, 1969.

Townsend, Robert. *Up the Organization*. New York: Ballantine, 1978.

Webster, Fred A. ed. *Webster's Comprehensive Marketing Bibliography*. Kawkawlin, MI: Data Publisher, 1986.

Weitzen, H. Skip. *Telephone Magic*. New York: McGraw-Hill, 1986.

INDEX